Unless Recalled Earl

Work and Welfare in
Economic Theory

Work and Welfare in Economic Theory

Ugo Pagano

Basil Blackwell

First published 1985

Basil Blackwell Ltd
108 Cowley Road, Oxford OX4 1JF, UK

Basil Blackwell Inc.
432 Park Avenue South, Suite 1505,
New York, NY 10016, USA

British Library Cataloguing in Publication Data

Pagano Ugo
　　Work and welfare in economic theory.
　　1. Work
　　I. Title
　　306'.36'.01　　HD6955

ISBN 0-631-13728-9

Library of Congress Cataloging in Publication Data

Pagano, Ugo, 1951–
　　Work and welfare in economic theory.

　　Bibliography: p.
　　Includes index.
　　1. Work. 2. Value. 3. Division of labor.
　　4. Economics. I. Title.
HD4904.P25　　1985　　　　330.1　　　　85–754

ISBN 0-631-13728-9

Typset by Unicus Graphics Ltd
Printed in Great Britain by The Camelot Press Ltd, Southampton

To the memory of my grandfather, Giorgio Focas

Contents

Preface

This book, which is based on a PhD dissertation at the University of Cambridge, had a limited circulation as a publication of the University of Siena Institute of Economics. A number of very useful comments and suggestions received at that stage have been taken into consideration in what follows.

I owe many thanks to Bob Rowthorn who, as my supervisor at the University of Cambridge, was always ready to listen and advise. It is hard for me to imagine how I could have written the present work without his encouragement and suggestions. Lynne Pepall often helped me to clarify my ideas and she has had a great influence on my way of thinking. I am very grateful to Marcello de Cecco for giving me moral and intellectual support ever since I was his student at the University of Siena. I have also received useful suggestions from my friend, Louis Makowski.

I wish to thank all my colleagues at the University of Siena, especially A. Cristofaro, M. di Matteo, R. M. Goodwin, B. Miconi, R. Paladini, F. Petri, L. Punzo, M. Tomveronachi, P. Puccinelli and M. L. Ruiz for having created a friendly atmosphere of 'intellectual exchange'.

I am indebted for the same reason to the members of the 'Italian Community' at Cambridge. In particular, I wish to thank S. Biasco (who can be considered the 'dean' of this community), F. Donzelli, M. Franzini, M. Leita and V. Termini. I also thank the Acton Society Trust and in particular Edward Goodman for letting me participate in their stimulating activities. Parts of chapters 7 and 9 have been published in the *Manchester School*: for their useful comments I wish to thank M. Amendola, G. Harcourt, J. Stiglitz and an anonymous referee of that journal.

This work was presented at a meeting of the CNR Group on the general theories of economics where I received interesting comments. I wish in particular to thank A. Montesano, P. Tani and S. Zamagni for organizing and participating at this meeting. I have also received useful comments from S. Bowles, A. Graziani, F. H. Hahn, A. Leijonhufvud, D. M. Nuti, L. L. Pasinetti, J. Roemer, I. Steedman, my colleague and friend A. Vercelli and an anonymous referee for Basil Blackwell. I was able to exploit only some of these comments directly; others simply made me more aware of the limits of my own work. Finally, I want to thank Bobbie Coe for typing this work on the computer, Jane Kenriek for improving my English and Sue Hughes for copy-editing the typescript. The responsibility for any mistakes is, of course, mine.

Introduction

In 1975, I wrote an essay on the economic theory of socialism. A survey of the literature at that time instilled in me a certain feeling of uneasiness, arising from the gap existing between the idea of socialism espoused by many of us involved in the students' movement of the late 1960s and the idea of socialism as conceptualized in orthodox economic theory.

My uneasiness arose mainly from two characteristics of orthodox economic theory. First, work, the nature and the transformation of which were so important to us, was treated in the economic theory of socialism – and also, more generally, in the theory of the allocation of resources – exactly in the same way as, say, steel and iron. In other words, human labour was treated as a resource, the use of which affected people's welfare only indirectly, through the production of consumption goods (including leisure) obtained by employing it. The second source of uneasiness was that different institutional forms of organizing production and coordinating the division of labour seemed to have little effect, or even, under certain assumptions, no effect, on the relation between work and welfare. The independent worker, the employee of a capitalist firm and the member of a socialist self-managed cooperative – all seemed to be using the same techniques and organization of production in their work.

Such a feeling of uneasiness suggested the following questions: How are work and welfare related? Could the institutional differences between market and non-market types of organizations (for instance, firms) be better stated? And were my two reasons for uneasiness related? Were some of the differences and relative merits of alternative institutions overlooked because the preferences of people for different uses of their work were not satisfactorily taken into account? Or, conversely, were the preferences of the workers not important because the firms were not considered

1

to be institutions alternative to, or anyway different from, the market? How could production be organized in order to improve the welfare of the workers?

The aim of the present book is to evaluate the answers that economists from Smith onwards have given to these questions and then to ask myself the questions once again.

The 'natural' starting point of this work has been an examination of the division of labour existing in the celebrated pin-making factory. In spite of the fact that this factory is linked to the name of Adam Smith, Smith was largely unable to understand that the division of labour was coordinated, in the case of his own celebrated example, by means other than the market. In the first chapter, the analyses of Gioia, Babbage and Ure are shown to be superior to that of Smith in this respect. They explain the division of labour with the principle of minimizing training time – a principle that a profit-maximizing employer necessarily follows when he or she decides how to organize the labour process. By contrast, it will be argued that Smith better understands the disadvantages of the division of labour within the factory – an insight that is directly linked to his conception of work, and in general of human activity.

The first aim of chapter 2 is to contrast the Smithian concept of work, and in general of economic activity, with that of the Ricardian school. Smith and Ricardo are often classified together under the label of 'classical' economists. From the point of view of the present work, however, they tend to lie at opposite poles. Smith is well aware of the fact that the welfare of people is affected by the kinds of activities they perform at work; Ricardo, on the other hand, believes that the use of labour to bring about the production of consumption goods is the only link between work and welfare, and he regards labour as an homogeneous activity that can be measured satisfactorily in hours. These different approaches of Smith and Ricardo are shown to imply not only a fundamental difference between their theories of value, but also a difference in their evaluation of the issue of the division of labour. While Smith is aware of the unsatisfactory consequences of a very detailed division of labour on the worker's welfare, Mill, a leading member of the Ricardian school, explicitly deduces from the assumption of homogeneous labour the consequence that a more detailed division of labour can only improve social welfare. A second aim of this chapter is to evaluate the contribution of those economists who have been called either Ricardian or, more recently, Smithian socialists, because of the influence that Ricardo or Smith was considered to have on their approach. In the present work these economists are divided into Smithian and Ricardian socialists. This classification is shown not to be purely a matter of terminology. In a socialist society the Smithian approach did not allow any objective evaluation of work independent of the tastes of the workers. By contrast, the 'true' Ricardian socialists deduced from the assumption of homogeneous labour that it was possible to calculate (labour-embodied) values independently of market exchange, and to reform the market in such a way that only just exchanges of equal quantities of (embodied) labour were carried out.

The starting point of chapter 3 is Marx's critique of the Ricardian model of socialism. Marx observes that the Ricardian socialist society will be simply unable to coordinate economic decisions because the society's reform prevents the market from achieving an equilibrium. The main purpose of this chapter, however, is to evaluate Marx's own models of a socialist society. I shall show that two contrasting models of an alternative society to capitalism can be found in the work of Marx and Engels. Unlike Smith, a great analytical merit of Marx lies in his full awareness that under capitalism the division of labour can be, and is in fact, coordinated by means other than the market. The firm conceived as a coordinating mechanism alternative to the market is shown to be the right key for understanding the two Marxian societies. The first model (single-firm socialism) extends the characteristics of firm-type coordination (planning, authority of the employer and so on) to society taken as a whole. The second model (anti-firm communism) is developed through a critique of the objectives and the division of labour carried out by the profit-maximizing firm. Marx did not perceive the contradiction between the two models because he believed that single-firm socialism should evolve smoothly into anti-firm communism. This belief is criticized in the last section of this chapter. There, Marx is also criticized for his undervaluation of some relative advantages of market-type coordination.

The purpose of chapter 4 is to compare (within the framework of a simple model) Marx's view of the economic process with that of the Ricardian school. In the Ricardian model the 'end' of society is to consume as many goods as possible. Workers are assumed to not have preferences for the kind of work that they perform; consequently, the human activity of production is conceived to be only a 'means' for achieving the goal of consumption, and is never conceived as well as an 'end' in itself. Marx criticizes the Ricardian school for taking these characteristics of economic activities, which occur, according to him, only under specific institutional frameworks (e.g. capitalism and single-firm socialism), as general definitional characteristics of economic activity; he does not believe in this separation of human activity into 'means and ends'. It is shown here that within the Marxian model it is possible to give an endogenous definition of work (i.e. where human activities are only means to an end). This difference between the Marxian and Ricardian definitions of work is shown to imply that the Marxian and Ricardian theories of value are also different. They become equal only when some restrictive assumptions are made defining a particular institutional framework. The Marxian model of communism is shown to be a good test of this difference.

The fifth chapter examines the English and the Austrian streams within the marginalist revolution. From the point of view of the present work, the approach of Jevons shares many aspects of the Smithian contribution. Jevons is well aware that the welfare of people is affected by the quality of their working life. His world of independent producers, who are free to determine the length and other aspects of their working life, is shown to be a more normative implication of his awareness than an analytical deficiency of a capitalist model. From the same point of view, Menger's approach is very close to that of the Ricardian school. His 'economic man' derives welfare only from the goods that he consumes, and he is indifferent to the kind of work that he performs.

These differences between the approaches of the founding fathers of the marginalist revolution explain well the reasons for the disputes about the 'ultimate standards of value' between their immediate successors in England and in Austria. Although these disputes have been largely forgotten, they are shown to be very interesting because they clarify certain welfare implications of different institutional arrangements, such as the employment relationship. Moreover, within the framework of these disputes Wieser develops the theory of opportunity cost and shows its implications for the economic theory of a communist society.

Chapter 6 is dedicated entirely to evaluating the contribution of Walras. The Walrasian system is usually interpreted as the description of an idealized competitive capitalist society. However, Walras intended to build a Utopian model of a perfect socialist society which could reconcile the aims of achieving social justice and maximizing social welfare. Like the Ricardian socialists, Walras looked for a world of just exchanges which could satisfy the requirement of commutative justice – a condition required by him for realizing distributive justice. He perceived that exchange and production decisions carried out at non-equilibrium prices would have prevented his perfect socialist from achieving both commutative justice and the maximization of social welfare. His 'ticket scheme' for an economy was an ambiguous way of coping with this problem. Such an economy is claimed here to be closer to the Marxian definition of a planned economy than to the actual features of the market.

Another characteristic of Walras's perfect society is that welfare is assumed to be affected directly by consumption goods and leisure, and only indirectly by work. The Walrasian formulation was a successful compromise between the approaches of Menger and Jevons. It has become the standard formulation in the modern textbooks of economics. However, it can be easily shown that including leisure and not (directly) work in the utility function is tantamount to assuming that workers are indifferent among different uses of their labour power. Therefore it is argued that the Walrasian leisure device is certainly a very misleading assumption in the framework of normative economics. Furthermore, it can hardly be used to define the characteristics of a 'perfect society'.

The purpose of chapter 7 is to criticize the rules that can be derived, and in fact are often derived, from the Walrasian leisure device. These rules are:

(1) Organize production by de-skilling jobs.
(2) Choose those techniques of production that are technologically efficient.
(3) Allocate labour within the firm according to the profit maximization maxim.

According to these rules, the authority of a profit-maximizing manager goes undisputed by the workers. Since to use the Walrasian leisure device is to ignore people's preferences for the allocation of their work, the derivation of such authoritarian and anti-democratic rules is hardly surprising. When workers' preferences are taken into account, these rules are shown to be inconsistent with the maximization of social welfare. In particular, no internal allocation of work within the profit-maximizing firm as such should be allowed; instead, the provisional conclusion of this chapter is that the allocation of labour should be handled either by an omniscient central planner who knows workers' preferences, or through market transactions taken at equilibrium prices.

In chapter 8 it is argued that these two alternatives ignore either the costs of using the market or the costs of using the planning mechanism. Two convergent streams in the recent literature are examined. The first arises from the observation that there are costs involved in using the market mechanism; it is argued therefore that some transactions should be internalized within the firm. The second stream begins with the consideration that there are costs involved in using the planning mechanism; it is argued therefore that some decisions should be decentralized to smaller sub-units as firms. Although the starting points are different, both streams of literature can be used together to justify the existence of firms' internal allocation.

The purpose of the concluding chapter is to investigate the possibility of conceiving an institutional arrangement that is capable of economizing on the cost of organizing production activity while at the same time considering the preferences of the workers. It is argued that these two aims could be achieved by organizations that maximize not only profits but also the utility that the workers derive from their work. In other words, the market cannot completely coordinate economic activity (because of the costs of using the market mechanism), and hence non-market organizations must exist in the economy; hence the utility function of the workers should be internalized by these non-market organizations. A similar argument is put forward for the case of planning. The conclusion of this book, therefore, is that economists should accept the fact that industrial democracy and workers' control are important, not simply as an end in themselves, but also because of their economic implications. Only an extension of democracy to working life can bring about an organization of work and the use of production techniques that are consistent with the needs of individuals as producers.

1
The division of labour and the pin-making problem

1 *The Smithian explanation*

In his paper, 'The Division of Labour in the Economy, the Polity and Society', Arrow (1979) criticizes Adam Smith for regarding the division of labour or the complementarity of skills as a peculiarly human trait. He notes that it is widely known, thanks to both common knowledge and science, that cooperative specialized behaviour is a major aspect of bees, ants and wasps. Smith, however, confines the division of labour to human beings, because he notices that animals never engage in exchange. Since Smith considers exchange to be the only means whereby the division of labour can be originated and the coordination of different kinds of work achieved, animals cannot enjoy the advantages of the division of labour.

'This is a deficiency of analysis', claims Arrow; 'Smith is apparently not aware of the possibility that interaction and cooperation can be achieved by other means than the market' (1979, p. 157). Arrow notes that, although the market is a very important coordination mechanism, it is also true that, if we take the social sphere as a whole, the market is simply one among other coordinating mechanisms. In his paper he is interested in assessing how self-interest and market-type coordination can be effective only if a certain degree of non-self-interested, non-market-type cooperation is present in society. It is very difficult to disagree with him. What I am interested in pointing out, however, is that Arrow's criticism of Adam Smith is so general that it can be made using Smith's own famous example of pin-making.

As is widely known, Smith used pin-making to illustrate what he claims to be the three advantages of the division of labour: improved dexterity, saving of time otherwise spent in changing occupations, and application of machinery invented by workmen thanks to their specialization in a particular field. It can be disputed that pin-making is a good example of Smith's three advantages, but I want first to concentrate on another point. The pin-making example certainly contradicts what Smith wants to show in the second chapter of the *Wealth of Nations*: that the division of labour of the members of society is coordinated only by the means of exchange.

'One man draws the wire, another straightens it, a third cuts it' is the famous beginning of Adam Smith's example (1976, p. 8). However, in this example the man who draws the wire does not *sell* it to the man who straightens it, and the latter does not *sell* the straightened wire to the man who cuts it. Smith's example shows exactly what Arrow maintains in opposition to Smith: that the market mechanism is not by any means the only one by which interaction and cooperation can be achieved. Smith does not seem to perceive the difference between this example and the one that he gives in the second chapter, in which he illustrates how, in a tribe of hunters or shepherds, a particular person specializes in producing bows and arrows and trades with other members of the tribe who specialize in the production of different goods. In such a tribe, a person who produces bows and arrows with greater dexterity and readiness finds it convenient to exchange them for cattle and venison, since 'he can in this way get more cattle and venison than if he himself went to the fields to catch them' (p. 19). In this second example, the coordinating mechanism described by Smith is really the market. Unlike the pin-making example, cattle and venison are *exchanged for* bows and arrows. Unlike the small pin factory that Smith had seen, 'where only ten men were employed' (p. 8), no employer is coordinating the distinct operations of the men of the tribe.

The Wealth of Nations can provide us with an explanation of how the market coordinates and favours the specialization of members of society, but its analytical power is not able to penetrate the doors of the pin factory. There, a type of coordination different from the one in which the tribe of self-employed hunters and shepherds operates, is working.

The pin factory in no way performs the indirect role that Adam Smith had given to it: that of showing the advantage of market-type coordination. What we now want to see is whether it plays the *immediate* role he assigned to it: that of showing the advantages of the division of labour. Let us consider these advantages in greater detail. Although he specified three such advantages, these can be really reduced to one: specialization increases job-specific skills, which in turn results in an improved performance in production. The first advantage specified by Smith (improved dexterity) and the third advantage (invention of new machines by workmen) can, in fact, be summarized by saying that specialization in a certain activity improves a worker's skill in producing a certain output with given machines and his skill of inventing better machines for producing that certain output. As to the second advantage (that concentration on a single occupation saves time that would otherwise be spent in changing occupations), Smith is aware of the fact that time wasted in switching from one occupation to another can be saved by concentrating all the occupational *locations* of a worker in a small area. The main reason for this, according to Smith, is that a satisfactory level of concentration in a certain activity is achieved only after a certain length of time: when first starting something we are still distracted by what we were doing before. This principle can thus again be related to the idea that specialization, by improving our concentration on a certain activity, also improves our ability to do it, and so favours job-specific skills.

In the Smithian tribe of hunters and shepherds, the individual who specialized in the production of bows and arrows seems to be a good example of someone who is able to exploit the three advantages of the division of labour. His dedication to bow and arrow-making improves his skill in making them; and dexterity, concentration and inventiveness are continuously improving the quantity and quality of his output, often suggesting to him new tools and machines that will improve his workmanship.

There is a lot of good common sense in Adam Smith's analysis of the advantages of the division of labour. Ultimately these advantages tell us what probably everyone believes: that if only we concentrate on a certain activity for a sufficient period of time will we be able to perform it satisfactorily. However, in spite of their good common sense, Smith's principles of the division of labour, together with market-type coordination, are bound to be outside the door of the pin-making factory that was meant to be an illustration of them. Let us imagine ourselves entering the factory and watching the man who cuts the wire. Since his task is very simple, after a short while his dexterity has stopped improving and is now only going to suffer through the debilitating effects of the monotony of the job. Even if working for only a short period, he thinks continuously of the hours he has spent the night before at the pub: the task he performs is too narrow and repetitive to arouse his interest and stimulate his concentration. As far as his inventiveness goes, this appears to be seriously damaged by his having to repeat the same simple, monotonous exercise for the entire working day. His attention and observation are restricted to a small part of the productive process; he is unable to hold an overall view of the process which is required for formulating innovations and inventing new machines. In order to obtain new machines, he has to rely exclusively on those 'machine-makers and philosophers' who can observe the entire process from outside and are equipped with scientific and technical tools.

Even a brief visit to the pin-making factory will persuade us that job-specific skills are much less important there than in the tribe of shepherds and hunters. We have seen how the person who makes bows and arrows in the tribe is a good example of somebody who acquires a job-specific skill. Let us, however, perform with him a conceptual experiment: let us make a film of his activity and then cut it into single frames. We shall see that, in order to make a single movement contained in one frame of the movie, no job-specific skill will be needed; all will require the same simple skills, namely, the ability to move one's hand in different directions. If we assign to each worker the task of making one of the movements contained in each frame, we can produce the bows and arrows without any job-specific skill (except that of the film director). This demonstrates how extreme specialization is associated with the absence of job-specific skill. That is the opposite of the Adam Smith type of specialization, whose advantages rely precisely on job-specific skills. The pin-making factory is at least halfway between the hunters- and shepherds-type of specialization and 'extreme' specialization. For this reason, not only market-type coordination but also the three advantages of the division of labour are bound to be largely outside its gates.

2 Alternative explanations

2.1 Gioia

In his long book, *Nuovo Prospetto delle Scienze Economiche*, published in 1815, the Italian economist Mechiorre Gioia makes the same criticism of Adam Smith as that recently made by

Arrow (Gioia, 1815, p. 115). This does not of course diminish the importance of Arrow's criticism; many people still hold the same view as Smith, and, in fact, Arrow associates Smith and Rawls in the same criticism.

Gioia not only points out how the division of labour exists in the animal world and in the human world independently of exchange, but he also criticizes Adam Smith for not having understood that cooperation has considerable advantages even if it is not associated with the complementarity of skills or the division of labour. The association of qualitatively equal kinds of labour increases efficiency in production: each person who cooperates in production with $n-1$ people would obtain much less than $1/n$ of the desired effect if he decided to work alone; alternatively, he would have to put in much more than n times the same effort if he wanted to obtain the same result alone. Gioia gives various examples of this principle, which he takes from both the animal and human world. In one of them he mentions the case of the cranes who, by flying in a triangle, meet much less air resistance (Gioia, 1815, p. 117). Cranes are also used in order to illustrate a second advantage of association: some effects, which are impossible for isolated human beings or animals, become possible when they operate as a group. For this reason, when the wind becomes strong and threatens to break their triangle, the cranes form a very tight circle: without this precaution (impossible in the case of a single crane) they would no longer obtain the desired effect, namely, flying in a certain direction.

Gioia next examines the reasons that make not only convenient but even necessary the division of labour within an association. His major line of thought is as follows. We start from the idea that different jobs require different levels of strength and/or skill, and that different members of the association are endowed with various degrees of skill and strength. People who possess a higher degree of skill and/or strength are the only ones who can dedicate themselves to the occupations that require a higher degree of skill and/or strength; it follows that the other members of the association will have to dedicate themselves to the occupations requiring a lower level of strength and/or skill (Gioia, 1815, pp. 129-30). Moreover, since skill is largely acquired, specialization of the members of the associations saves training time (p. 132). The more the members of the association specialize, the greater is their time saved in acquiring skills and the more time can be dedicated to producing useful goods. This is the main reason why, according to Gioia, the division of labour is one of the sources of the wealth of nations.

2.2 *Babbage*

In the preface to his book, *On the Economy of Machinery and Manufacturers* (1832), Babbage writes that 'several of the principles that I have proposed, appear to me to have been unnoticed before. This was particularly the case with regard to the explanation I have given of the division of labour; but further inquiry satisfied me that I have been anticipated by M. Gioia . . .'. (p. v.)

This generous acknowledgement should not be taken too literally. Babbage enables us to take a decisive step towards understanding the features of the coordination and division of labour within the factory. He explains how an employer can exploit the advantages of the division of labour which Gioia had previously illustrated. Babbage synthesizes his contribution to the understanding of the advantages of the division of labour in the following principle:

> That the master manufacturer, by dividing the work to be performed into different processes each requiring different degrees of skill and force, can purchase exactly that precise quantity necessary for each process; whereas, if the entire work is executed by one workman, that person must possess sufficient skill to perform the most difficult, and sufficient strength to carry out the most laborious of the operations into which the art is divided. (Babbage, 1832, pp. 137–8)

On the basis of this principle, Babbage provides an alternative explanation of the division of labour in pin-making:

> The art of making needles is, perhaps, that which I would have selected as including a very large number of processes all remarkably different in their nature; but the less difficult art of pin-making has some claim for attention, having been used for his illustration of the subject by Adam Smith. (Babbage, 1832, p. 138)

Babbage makes a very detailed and interesting exposition of the organization of work in the pin-making factory. However, in order to understand how his principle explains the division of labour within the factory, we can concentrate on the first two productive processes of pin-making and accept one of his empirical results: drawing the wire requires a skill greater than straightening it. Let us now assume that the master manufacturer has not divided the drawing and straightening of the wire into two different processes and that he employs two people, each of whom performs both tasks. The two workmen must have a degree of skill at least equal to that required by the most difficult of the two processes (i.e., drawing the wire). The wages of both of these workers (Babbage assumes that wages are an increasing function of skill) therefore will be at least as high as the wage paid to a workman who is able to draw the wire.

Let us now see what happens if the master manufacturer decides to divide the work into two different processes and employs one worker to draw the wire and another to straighten it. While he has to pay the worker who draws the wire exactly (and not at least) according to the skill required for doing it, he can certainly pay less to the worker who merely straightens the wire. The skill required for the latter task is, in fact, certainly less than the skill required either for performing the two processes or for only drawing the wire. Thus, simple cost-minimizing behaviour makes the master manufacturer divide the work into different processes and assign them to different workers. A hierarchy is created in the set of jobs performed in the factory according to their skill requirement. At the bottom of the hierarchy, the jobs do not require any job-specific skill: only some general skills, such as the ability to move one's hands in a certain direction, are required. This consequence of the division of labour can be contrasted with Adam Smith's view of the advantages of the division which rely on the fact that it favours the development of job-specific skills. If we refer to the jobs at the bottom of the hierarchy, the advantages of the division of labour seem to rely on the opposite consequences: that it is possible to create a vast number of jobs that do *not* require any specific skill.

2.3 Ure

A contemporary of Babbage, A. Ure, comes to the conclusion outlined above. However, in arriving at this conclusion he relies mainly on a different characteristic of the factory system: the introduction of machinery. In his book, *The Philosophy of Manufactures*, written in 1835, he notes that, at the time when Adam Smith wrote 'his immortal elements of economics, automatic machinery being hardly known', he was properly led to regard the division of labour as the grand principle of manufacturing improvement, and that Smith showed, in the pin-making example, how 'each craftsman, by being able to perfect one point by practice, became a quicker and cheaper workman' (Ure, 1835, p. 19).

However, what precisely worries Ure in the pin-making factory is that a Smithian type of job-specific skill is still necessary for carrying out some productive processes. While he is perfectly happy about the wire-cutting job, which requires no skill, he notes that the formation and fixation of the pin-heads is comparatively difficult and that a higher wage has to be paid to the man doing the latter job. 'But', claims Ure, 'what was in Dr Smith's time a topic of useful illustration, can not now be used without the risk of misleading the public's mind as to the right principle of the manufacturing industry' (p. 19). In fact, the division, or rather the adaptation, of labour to the different talents of men is little thought of in factory employment:

> On the contrary, wherever a process requires particular dexterity and steadiness of hand, it is withdrawn as soon as possible from the 'cunning' workman who is prone to many kinds of irregularities, and it is placed in charge of a particular mechanism, so self-regulating that a child could supervise it. (Ure, 1835, p. 19)

A workman's job-specific skill, which Adam Smith considers as the source of the wealth of nations, is not only useless in the factory but even damaging, once this skill is not needed. Ure notes that 'the more skilful the workman, the more self-willed and intractable he is apt to become and, of course, the less fit for being a component of a mechanical system where, by occasional irregularities, he can do great damage to the whole' (p. 20). He quotes as an example the case of a certain Mr Anthony Strutt, who directed a cotton factory and who would no longer employ anyone who had learned his craft by regular apprenticeship. Moreover, Ure claims that he was told by 'an eminent mechanic in Manchester' that 'he does not choose to make any steam-engines at present, because with his existing means, he would have to resort to the old principle of the division of labour' (p. 21) – that is, to the principle that Adam Smith believed to be so advantageous.

3 Pin-making now and Babbage's predictions

Let us now take a big jump forward in time and revisit one of the two firms who produce pins in Britain today. (For this purpose

I have used Pratten, 1980.) Over the last 200 years productivity has increased 167 times. The division of labour on the shop floor has been actually abolished: jobs have become so simple that they can be rotated. Differences in wages at the bottom of the hierarchy have been either abolished or reduced (for adult employees the ratio of the highest paid to the lowest paid is now less than 1.5 to 1; while the range given by Babbage was 6 to 1). However, a hierarchy of technical and administrative staff with relatively high incomes, which has no counterpart in either Adam Smith's or Charles Babbage's time, now exists in the pin-making factory.

The creation of a hierarchy of skills with no job-specific skills at the bottom is perfectly consistent with the Babbage principle and with Ure's view of the role of the introduction of machinery. Smith's advantages of the division of labour *per se* are denied, as Pratten points out (1980, p. 95), by the recent experiments in job rotation on the shop floor,[1] and the advantages of job-specific skills are a characteristic only of some manual workers (like maintenance mechanics) and some clerks.

As to clerks, Babbage had already noted that his principle applied to clerical work as well. Babbage, who held the Lucasian Professorship of Mathematics at the University of Cambridge and dedicated a large part of his life to the realization of computing machines, gives an example from his professional field. Immediately after the 1789 revolution, the French government wanted to produce a series of mathematical tables which would facilitate the extension of the decimal system which they had recently adopted. M. Prony, who was in charge of this undertaking, organized the production of these tables according to the same principle applied (according to Babbage) to the pin-making firm: he divided the workers at the tables into three sections. The duty of the first section, which consisted of five or six of the most eminent French mathematicians, was to 'investigate among the various analytical expressions which could be found for the same functions, that most readily adaptable to simple numerical calculation by many individuals employed at the same time. This section had little or nothing to do with the actual numerical work' (Babbage, 1832, p. 156). The second section 'consisted of seven or eight people of considerable acquaintance with mathematics; and their duty was to convert into numbers the formulae put into their hands by the first section – an operation of great labour – and to deliver these formulae to the members of the third section, and receive from them the finished calculations. The members of this section had certain means of verifying these calculations without the necessity of repeating or even examining the entire work done by the third section' (p. 156). The members of the third section, 'whose number varied from sixty to eighty, received certain numbers from the second section, and using nothing more than simple addition and subtraction, they returned the finished tables to that section' (p. 156).

Babbage explains that nine-tenths of the third class had no knowledge of arithmetic beyond the two simple rules exercised for making the tables. The saving of skill, which is the application of the principle formulated by Babbage, is fairly impressive in this example of 'division of mental labour'. However, it is even more striking that Babbage can forecast which division of labour will emerge as a result of the introduction of the 'calculating engine' that he was trying to construct. He anticipates that three new sections will be formed (Babbage, 1832, pp. 157–8). The first includes the people who are actually capable of designing the 'calculating engine', the second is formed by engineers who are able to operate the machines, some of whom should understand the nature of the processes to be carried out, and the third comprises those who are only able to use the 'calculating engines'. However, the fact that the use of modern computers usually involves a division of labour in which at least four sections can be distinguished within Babbage's third section, and of which the bottom section is required only to key-punch, shows how much further the Babbage principle has been applied in our day and age.

The Babbage principle has a further advantage. It enables us to understand the extent to which the division of labour within the factory can be independent of the market, which Smith believed to be the only coordinating system. We have already noticed that, within the factory, workers do not sell or buy the products of their labour, and that it is the employer who ensures that there is a consistent production plan and that the separate parts of the productive process are correctly proportioned. Yet, it may be argued that the market does have a coordinating role in so far as the employer has to buy the skill of the worker who performs the different productive processes in the labour market. However, it can easily be seen that, in spite of this argument, the division of labour can be decided inside the factory without any knowledge of or consideration for the labour market. In fact, since Babbage assumes that, whatever the relative wages are, the latter are always an increasing function of skill, it is always convenient for the employer to divide the production processes into 'finer' jobs involving the performance of fewer tasks and therefore a lower degree of skill and lower wages.

The division of labour within the firms appears in this way to be completely independent of the market system. It also appears to be independent of the kind of society in which it is performed. It seems to be a rather simple rule by which we can economize on the human skills and strength necessary for the production of wealth. However, some disturbing consequences of this simple rule did not escape the careful eye of Adam Smith. In the fifth book of the *Wealth of Nations* he notes:

> In the progress of the division of labour, the employment of the far greater part of those who live by labour, that is of the great body of the people, comes to be confined to a few very simple operations: frequently one or two. But the understanding of the greater part of mankind is necessarily formed by their ordinary employment. The man whose life is spent in performing a few simple operations of which the effects upon one are, perhaps, always the same, or at least very nearly the same, has no occasion to exert his understanding or exercise his inventiveness for discovering expedients for removing difficulties which never occur. Therefore, he naturally loses the habit of such exertion, and generally becomes as stupid and ignorant as it is possible for a human creature to become. The torpor of his mind renders him not only incapable of relishing or bearing a point in any rational conversation, but also of conceiving any generous, noble or tender sentiments, and consequently of forming any just judgment concerning many of even the most ordinary duties of private life. (Smith, 1976, pp. 302–3)

While the latter observations sound like an acknowledgement of the failure of the three advantages of the division of labour as a tool for understanding the manufacturing world, they open the gates of the factory to the criticism of the division of labour that is suggested by Ure and Babbage. The reason why Smith is able to understand so well the *disadvantages* of that factory world, of which he had so poorly understood the advantages, can be found in his conception of labour and, more generally, of human activities. An analysis of this is an indispensable tool for understanding how the division of labour proposed by Ure and Babbage can be criticized on the grounds that there is a better possible alternative.

For this reason, the next chapter is largely dedicated once again to Adam Smith.

Notes

1   Braverman (1974) maintains that de-skilling jobs is a general tendency of capitalism. His argument is based on the Babbage principle. He also argues that a de-skilling job strategy is followed by capitalists for reasons of control and power. De-skilling jobs enables the employers to have the complete control of the labour process, while making the workers easily replaceable and dependent on the skills of management. I find the 'Babbage principle' argument convincing (at least in situations where workers' resistance to the employers' strategies is weak). On the other hand, I believe that the 'control' argument can either reinforce (as Braverman maintains) or weaken and even, sometimes, invert the de-skilling strategy of the employers. In some situations employers can increase discipline and productivity of some groups of workers by involving them in their jobs and in factory life – a strategy that may imply *re*skilling (or, at least, not de-skilling) jobs. The second strategy (and the circumstances under which it occurs) has been examined by Friedman (1977), Edwards (1979), Littler (1982) and Sabel (1982).

2
Smithian labour and Ricardian socialism

1 *Smith v. Ricardo*

Karl Marx observed in the 1840s that, 'not only does political economy become increasingly cynical from Smith through Say to Ricardo, Mill etc. . . . the latter becomes more estranged from man than their predecessors' (Marx, 1975, p. 343).

More than 40 years later, A. Marshall was to make a similar remark about Smith and the Ricardian school. Regarding the former, Marshall maintained that Smith's most important contribution was not his famous argument that 'government does harm by interfering in trade'; rather, 'his chief work was to indicate the manner in which value measures human motive' (Marshall, 1885, p. 157). The approach of the Ricardian school, on the contrary, was seriously handicapped by the fact that their conception of man 'led them to regard labour simply as a commodity without throwing themselves into the point of view of the workman: without allowing for his human passions, his instincts and habits, his sympathies and antipathies, his class jealousies and class adhesiveness, his want of knowledge and of the opportunities for free and vigorous action' (p. 155).

We have seen how Smith criticized some of the consequences of the division of labour within the firm. The Ricardian school not only completely accepted the organization of labour within the firm, but even showed, together with Mill, that the application of the Babbage principle to society as a whole always improved human welfare. The latter conclusion recalls very closely Gioia's contribution about the advantages of the division of labour.

The aim of the following section is to show that these different conclusions of Smith and the Ricardian school are deeply rooted in their value theories and their conception of man, whose profound differences have been put forward so well by Marx and Marshall as in the passages quoted above. The final section of this chapter examines the theories of those economists who are named either 'Ricardian socialists' or, more recently, 'Smithian socialists', because of the influence that Smith and Ricardo has had on their theories. According to the difference noted above, a new classification of these authors into Smithian and Ricardian socialists is suggested. Finally, the contributions of the 'Smithian and Ricardian socialists' to the economic theory of socialism are evaluated.

2   *Labour and value*

2.1   *Smith*

In the preceding chapter we saw how Adam Smith failed to appreciate the difference between the division of labour existing in the tribe of hunters and that existing in a society where production is carried out in pin-making and similar manufacturing firms. On the other hand, when the author of the *Wealth of Nations* comes to explain market values, he makes a clear distinction between an independent workers' society (like that of the tribe of hunters) and the situation in which the workers are employed in pin-making types of firms. According to Smith, the first occurs in the 'early and rude' state of society before the accumulation of stock and the appropriation of land; in this case the whole product of work belongs to the workers. The second situation occurs in a more advanced state of society after stock has been accumulated and is used in production and land has been appropriated by private owners; in this case a part of the product is appropriated by the owner of stocks as profit and by the landowners as rent.

Let us begin by examining Smith's explanation of exchange relations in that 'early and rude state' of society in which all the product of labour belongs to the worker. In this case 'the quantity' of labour necessary for acquiring different objects seems to be the only factor that can afford a rule for exchanging them for one another (Smith, 1976, p. 53). If in Adam Smith's tribe of hunters 'it usually costs twice the labour to kill a beaver than it does to kill a deer, one beaver should exchange for or be worth two deer. It is natural that what is usually the produce of two days' or two hours' labour, should be worth double of what is usually the produce of one day's or one hour's labour' (p. 53). However, even in the 'early and rude state of society', the labour theory of value is subject to two important exceptions, arising from the nature of labour itself. Immediately after putting forward his classic deer–beaver example, Smith notices how labour time is non-homogeneous since different types of labour are characterized by different degrees of hardship and skill requirements.

Non-homogeneity of labour time has a crucial relevance in the *Wealth of Nations*. In another famous passage Smith states that 'the real price of everything, what everything really costs to the man who wants to acquire it, is the toil and trouble of acquiring it' (1976, p. 34). Smith refers to toil and trouble and not to hours of work, because he believes that different hours of work do, in general, contain different amounts of toil and trouble. 'There may be more labour', he maintains, 'in one hour's hard work than in two hours of easy business, or in an hour's application to a trade which it cost ten year's labour to learn, than in a month's industry at an ordinary and obvious employment' (p. 35). The difficulty of measuring labour explains why, 'though labour be the real measure of the exchangeable value of all commodities, it is not that by which their value is commonly estimated' (p. 35).

On the contrary, labour is continuously estimated 'in exchanging the different productions of different sorts of labour for one other', as some allowance is commonly made for both hardship and ingenuity. It is adjusted, however, not by any accurate measure but by the 'higgling' and bargaining of the market, 'according to that sort of rough equality which though not exact is sufficient for carrying on the business of common life'.

The importance of the non-homogeneity of labour time in the *Wealth of Nations* can, however, be fully appreciated only if we leave for a while the 'early and rude' state of society and move to chapter 10, where Smith examines the causes of wages and profit differentials in their different employments in a more advanced state of society. The first of these causes is considered by Smith to be the 'disagreeableness or agreeableness' of the different employments. Looking back from his age to the 'early and rude state' of society, Smith observes how 'hunting and fishing, the most important employments of mankind in the rude state of society, become in its advanced state their most agreeable amusements, and they pursue for pleasure what they once followed from necessity' (Smith, 1976, p. 113).

In conclusion, we can say that, in Adam Smith's conception, labour cannot be either defined or measured objectively. Society's tastes, together with society's technology, determine through the market mechanism whether hunting and fishing are to be defined as labour time or as amusements. Moreover, any objective measure of labour is handicapped by the fact that different kinds of employment of the same kind of labour are characterized by different levels of agreeableness according to certain given tastes of society. Even in the 'early and rude' state of society, prices of goods are proportional to the 'toil and trouble' that is required for producing them, and not simply to labour time.

If we leave the primitive state of society and consider a society where capital stock has been accumulated and land is privately owned, then, according to Smith, 'in this state of things, the whole produce of labour does not always belong to the labourer', since he must share it with the owner of the stock that employs him and the landlord. In this case, the quantity of labour commonly employed in acquiring or producing any commodity is not anymore 'the only circumstance which can regulate the quantity which ought commonly to purchase, command or exchange for' (1976, p. 55). 'An additional quantity, it is evident, must be due for the profits of the stock which advanced the wages and furnished the materials of that labour' (p. 55). Moreover, 'as soon as the land of any country has all become private property, the landlords like all other men love to reap where they never sowed, and demand a rent even for its natural produce' (p. 56).

For Smith, therefore, only in a hunting type of society is the toil and trouble, or the labour, that is required to produce goods the *only* circumstance that regulates exchange. In the contemporary world of pin-making (etc.) firms it is very clear to Smith that the value of the product of labour (or the quantity of labour that the product can 'command') is considerably superior to the labour that is 'embodied' in it. Profits and rents are the difference between these two values.

2.2 *Ricardo*

Ricardo's theory of value differs from the Smithian one in two major aspects. On the one hand, Ricardo maintains that the costs that men incur in acquiring useful commodities can be objectively estimated in units of time. On the other hand, he extends (although with some exceptions) the domain of the labour theory of value, as a tool for explaining relative prices, to the 'advanced state of society' in which land has been appropriated and stocks have been accumulated in private hands. He completely ignores the fact that different units of labour-time can be differently agreeable to the members of society and that disagreeableness is a fundamental element in defining labour-time itself. Not taking into consideration this fundamental Smithian concern, Ricardo is left with only one possible cause of the non-homogeneity of labour: a difference in skill content. Ricardo is not worried about this problem, however. He believes that the evaluation of different skills can be assumed to be fairly stable in the market economy in comparison with the movement of the relative prices of the products of labour. On the other hand, he explicitly states in his 'Notes on Malthus' (1953) the values of different kinds of skilled labour can be estimated objectively by computing the average training time that is necessary in acquiring them. In this way skilled labour can be reduced to a certain quantity of unskilled labour even independently of any information about wage differentials.

Either having not considered the matter of whether labour is meaningfully measurable or even definable in time units, or having solved the problem that can make labour not meaningfully measurable or even definable in time units, Ricardo criticizes Adam Smith's distinction between his 'early and rude state of society' and the society of his own age. Even in that early state to which Smith refers, Ricardo maintains that some capital, though possibly made and accumulated by the hunter himself, would be necessary to enable him to kill his game. Without some weapon, neither the beaver or the deer could be destroyed, and therefore the value of these animals would be regulated not solely by the time and labour necessary for their actual destruction but also by the time and labour necessary for providing the hunter's capital, namely, the weapon by the aid of which their destruction was effected (Ricardo, 1971, p. 66). In both the 'early state' and the 'advanced' state of society, the labour theory of value has to be modified in order to take into account the fact that 'not only the labour applied immediately to commodities affects their value, but also that which is bestowed on the implements, tools and buildings with which such labour is assisted' (p. 65). 'Exchange values are in proportion to the labour bestowed on their production; not on their immediate production only, but on all those implements or machines required to give effect to the particular labour to which they were applied' (p. 67).

Thus Adam Smith has failed to understand that 'capital' is used in both the early and the advanced state of society, and this simply implies that the quantity of labour that is employed in producing it must also be taken into account in both cases. As far as land is concerned, Ricardo uses the opposite argument: rent does not affect the labour theory of value in either the early state of society or its advanced state. In both cases, on the marginal land exchange value is proportional to the labour bestowed in production. Rent is only compensating the circumstance that the average productivity of labour is higher on the non-marginal pieces of land that are cultivated. The conclusion is, again, that no meaningful distinction can be made between the way in which exchange values are regulated in the 'early' state of society and in modern society. Thus the labour theory of value, according to Ricardo, not only can overcome (or forget) the problems that arise from non-homogeneous labour, but also can be considered a proper explanation of the exchange relations of any society.

2.3   James Mill

The labour theory of value, and in particular the homogeneity of labour, has a clear implication for the problems concerning the division of labour that we have examined in the preceding chapter. This implication will be put forward by a friend and disciple of Ricardo: James Mill.

In his *Elements of Political Economy* (1844), Mill argues that the end of the economic system is to consume as many goods as possible. 'Political Economy', he maintains, 'is to the State what domestic economy is to the family'.

> The family consumes; and in order to consume is must supply. Domestic economy has therefore, two grand objects: the consumption and supply of the family. Consumption being a quantity always indefinite, for there is no end to the desire for enjoyment, the grand concern is to increase supply. It thus appears that four inquiries are included in this science: 1st – what are the laws according to which the production of commodities are regulated; 2nd – what are the laws through which the commodities produced by the labour of the community are distributed; 3rd – what are the laws according to which commodities are exchanged; and 4th – what are the laws which regulate consumption. (Mill, 1844, p. 4)

Mill conceives economic activity as having an end in consumption and a starting point in production. As to the latter, very simple normative rules can be stated considering that (1) the end of production is to produce the maximum possible number of consumption goods; and (2) the labour, which is the 'real cost of the real price' to society in order for the latter goods to be produced, is homogeneous, as in Ricardo's theory. The homogeneity of labour is justified by Mill in the following way. 'It is found', he argues, 'that the agency of man can be traced to very simple elements. He does nothing but produce motion. He can move things towards one another, and he can separate them from one another' (Mill, 1844, p. 5). In order for 'human motion' to be used in the best way, Mill maintains that two 'philosophical operations' have to be performed; 'the most philosophical analysis of the subject would be the first operation to be performed; the next would be an equally perfect philosophical synthesis' (p. 13). The first operation is done by decomposing the labour required for a certain purpose into its simple elements, while the second lies in combining the latter elements 'as means towards our ends' (p. 14).

Since 'a certain immense aggregate of operations is subservient to the production of the commodities useful and agreeable to man' (p. 11), Mill comes to the conclusion that 'it is of the highest importance that this aggregate should be divided into portions each consisting of as small a number of operations as possible ... (p. 11). The fact that performing each operation well requires training time is indicated by Mill as being the reason for the validity of the latter principle. It is easy to show that, given Mill's own assumptions (i.e., that maximum consumption is the end of production and labour is homogeneous), he is perfectly right.

The homogeneous labour required for producing each useful commodity can be divided into two parts: the time required for actually producing the commodity, and the time expended for learning the operations necessary for producing the commodity itself. For instance, let us assume that only two operations are necessary for producing each commodity and that a_1 and a_2 are the training times required for learning these operations. If n workers perform both operations, the total training time required is $n(a_1 + a_2)$. Let us now reorganize the production process, following Mill's suggestion that K workers ($K < n$) perform only the first operation and $n - K$ workers perform only the second operation. The total training time now required is $Ka_1 + (n - K)a_2$, which is obviously less than before. Because of this reduction of the training time required for learning the production operations, more time can now be dedicated to the actual production of useful commodities. Hence society can consume a greater number of commodities and achieve a higher level of welfare.

In conclusion, Mill suggests that the Babbage principle, which we considered in the preceding chapter, should be applied not only in the firm but more generally in the organization of society as a whole, in order that the welfare of all members of society can be increased. Mill's conclusions are in striking contrast with the theory outlined in the *Wealth of Nations*. First, Mill, like Babbage and Gioia, sees the advantages of the division of labour as lying more in the reduction of training time than in the increase in job-specific skills. Second, the division of labour is considered by Mill to be independent of exchange relations. Society finds the division of labour advantageous and organizes production according to the latter principle, like a 'big family'. In the family no exchange occurs. Moreover, trade is considered by Mill to be more a consequence than a cause of the division of labour (i.e., the opposite of Smith). Extreme division of labour requires large-scale production, and large-scale production requires an extensive market for the commodity produced.

Finally, Mill believes that an increase in specialization does not bring about any disadvantages of the type outlined in the *Wealth of Nations*. The increase in consumption, which is due to the decrease of training time, always causes an increase in social welfare. On the contrary, Smith sees as the main disadvantage of the division of labour the tedious nature of unskilled jobs which require no training, and he advocates an increase in state-financed education to offset their most damaging consequences. This latter difference from Mill's work can be attributed to the fact that Smith does not share the 'Ricardian school' assumption that labour is homogeneous 'human motion'. Workers are considered to have preferences about the allocation of their own work. They can suffer profoundly because of an extreme narrowing of the scope of their jobs. Increased specialization, which according to Mill necessarily increases society's welfare because it makes more consumption goods available, may decrease social welfare according to Smith because it increases the disutility of work. When the latter consideration is made, even the Babbage principle shows its hidden limits. Increased specialization could, in fact, increase manpower costs if 'manpower' feels that the job has become more boring and claims a wage increase for performing it in spite of the reduction in the training costs. No simple rule like the ones outlined by Babbage and Mill can be stated when the non-homogeneity of labour and the preferences of the workers are taken into account. 'Ricardian market values', expressing the quantity of homogeneous human motion that is required for the production of a commodity, necessarily fall when production is organized in such a way that each worker performs fewer tasks. On the contrary, 'Smithian values' do not necessarily fall when specialization is increased because the value of a commodity represents the amount of subjective 'toil and trouble' required for producing the commodity. This 'toil and trouble' could increase despite the reduction in training time.

3   Smithian and Ricardian socialists

3.1   Introduction

Ever since Foxwell's introduction to the book by the Austrian, Anton Menger (1899), those English economists who wrote in the 1820s and 1830s, maintaining the workers' right to the whole product of labour, have been called 'Ricardian socialists'. The latter denomination is usually meant to underline the fact that they drew socialist conclusions from the economic theories of Ricardo. According to this interpretation, the 'Ricardian socialists' derived their belief that workers have a natural right to the whole product of labour from the Ricardian theory according to which the value of a commodity depends entirely on the relative quantity of labour necessary for its production.

A. Ginsburg (1976) claims that this traditional interpretation cannot be held after a more careful investigation. None of these authors, he maintains, has ever argued that under capitalism values are proportional to the quantity of labour embodied in the commodities. N. Thompson (1981, p. 93) has added that some of these authors did rather maintain that under socialism values should be proportional to embodied labour, because they believe that the latter circumstances occurs only when the whole product of labour belongs to the workers. The latter situation resembles very closely the 'early and rude state' of society described by Smith, where capitalists and landowners are not entitled to any share of the product and the labour theory of value could explain exchange relations. The influence that these Smithian considerations have probably exercised on the belief of the 'Ricardian socialists' that there exists a 'natural state' where no exploitation occurs has suggested to Thompson that the 'Ricardian socialists' should be more appropriately called 'Smithian socialists'.

I hope I will not confuse readers too much in the following pages by arguing that, if these authors have to be classified according to their model of socialism, the term 'Ricardian socialist' should be reintroduced for some of them. A more detailed analysis of the 'Smithian and/or Ricardian socialists', Hodgskin, Thompson, Gray and Bray, is however necessary in order to try and solve this problem of terminology. This analysis is also useful for the more general reason that, as we will see in some later chapters, the debate about socialism in the 1820s and 1930s is at least as stimulating as the more recent and famous debate of the 1920s and 1930s. Furthermore, an analysis of the works of the 'Ricardian and/or Smithian socialists' is very important for understanding the models of socialism and communism that will be formulated by Marx starting from the limitations of their contributions.

3.2   *Hodgskin*

In his four lectures on *Popular Political Economy* delivered at the London Mechanics Institute, T. Hodgskin (1827) introduced a distinction between natural and social prices. The natural price of a commodity is the quantity of labour required to produce it; 'Nature exacted nothing but labour in time past, she demands only labour at present, and she will require merely labour in all future time' (p. 219). Reinforcing the well-known Smithian passage, Hodgskin adds that 'Labour was the original, is now and will be the only purchase money in dealing with Nature' (pp. 219–20).

The social price is the 'natural price enhanced by social regulations' (p. 220). In a sentence that closely recalls Adam Smith's description of the advanced state of society as contrasted with its 'early' state, Hodgskin notices that, 'whatever quantity of labour may be requisite to produce any commodity, the labourer must always, in the present state of society, give a great deal more labour to acquire and possess it than is requisite to buy it from nature. Natural price thus increased to the labourer is social price' (p. 220). 'Labour embodied' and 'labour commanded' have become natural and social prices in Hodgskin's reassessment. Workers have the right to fight for a society where only 'natural' prices are paid and the whole product of labour belongs to the labourer, as in Adam Smith's early state of society. However, Hodgskin himself, after having proposed in his *Labour Defended against the Claims of Capital* (1825) a model of a socialist or, better, an anarchist society, very similar to the Smithian state of society, notices that that model cannot in general determine the distribution of the product among the workers. 'If all kinds of labour were perfectly free ... there would be no difficulty on this point,' he maintains, 'and the wages individual labour would be justly settled by what Smith calls the "higgling of the market". Unfortunately labour is not, in general, free ...' (1825, p. 86).

The reason why Hodgskin argues that the Smithian 'higgling of the market' is an insufficient means for coordinating the work of society's members lies in his belief that, while in Adam Smith's early state a worker can kill a beaver or a deer alone, in general, commodities are produced jointly by various labourers. In Smith's early state, the implementation of the tenet that 'the whole produce of labour ought to belong to the labourer' would be hindered by ambiguity only because we have implicitly excluded the idea that cooperation is advantageous and sometimes necessary for achieving certain results. If the workers were always working freely and independently of each other, they could relate to one another only when exchanging the products of their labour. The amount of the product they ought to give in exchange in order to obtain the products of other workers could be determined by the higgling of the market. On the contrary, if more than one hunter is cooperating in order to kill the same deer or beaver, we are faced with the problem of finding a rule according to which the workers divide the product of joint labour. Hodgskin notices that, unfortunately,

> there is no principle or rule, as far as I know, for dividing the produce of joint labour among the different individuals who concur in production, but the judgement of the individuals themselves, that judgement depending on the value men may set on different species of labour can never be known, nor can any rule be given for its application by any single person. (Hodgskin, 1825, p. 83)

Hodgskin comes to the conclusion that it is impossible to decide how to distribute the products of joint labour unless 'by leaving it to be settled by the unfettered judgements of the labourers themselves' (1825, p. 85).

However, Hodgskin warns the labourers against two possible kinds of prejudices that may arise when the workers cooperate and perform different kinds of activities in order to exploit the advantages of the division of labour. The first involves the least useful parts of the social task being invested with great honour, while the second lies in 'a disposition to restrict labour to the operation of the hands' (1825, p. 86). The fact that the master-manufacturer does not perform manual operations in production, and that his wages 'have been blended with the profit of the capitalists' (p. 89), must not bring about the misunderstanding that masters are not labourers as well as their journeymen. They are also 'either capitalists or agents of the capitalists', but it would be a big mistake to forget that their knowledge and skill 'are just as necessary for the complete success of any complicated operation as the skill of the workmen whose hands actually alter the shape and fashion of the materials' (p. 88). Hodgskin does moreover stress that the growing level of instruction will make the knowledge and skill of the 'master-manufacturers' a decreasing scarce production factor in a future economy.

3.3 Thompson

W. Thompson's book (1827) was anonymously published as being by 'A member of the idle class'. The long title of the book – *Labour Rewarded: The Claims of Labour and Capital Conciliated, or How to Secure to Labour the Whole Products of its Exertions* – and its attribution immediately reveal its aim, which was to answer *Labour Defended against the Claims of Capital* by Hodgskin, who had signed his book as 'A labourer'.

Thompson begins by arguing that even members of the idle class like himself or Hodgskin (in spite of his self-denomination as 'a labourer'), and even some 'capitalists', perform some useful mental work, in spite of the fact that their activity does not increase material wealth. Thompson redefines labour as a *useful activity*, and maintains that 'useful activity or labour is that which, whether its immediate exercise be pleasurable or not, produces in its consequences a preponderance of good' (1827, p. 21). The principle according to which Thompson believes that workers should be rewarded is very simple: 'all species of cheerful exertion' should be 'equally remunerated' (p. 37). He criticizes the inequality of remuneration that arises from the higgling of the market for both moral and economic reasons. First, he believes

that equality of remuneration increases social welfare because of
a reformulated Benthian utilitarian rule; and, second, he notices
that, if each worker is entitled to the property of his product,
'the very old or young, the sick etc. would starve so that society
might run the risk of not being preserved' (p. 13).

By voluntarily agreeing before production to an equality of
remuneration, the members of society can ensure 'a vast increase
in production and enjoyment for everyone, as well as mutual
insurance from all casualties' (p. 37). The higgling of the market
is excluded by Thompson as a means for fixing the just remuneration of labour for 'economic' reasons too. He explicitly observes
that only 'an individual savage may himself fell the wood and kill
the animal necessary to supply the materials for his hut, his
clothing or his bow and may exchange, for what seems to him
good, these fabricated commodities, may ascertain in many cases
what are, and may therefore enjoy the entire use of the products
of labour' (p. 37). Thus Thompson is well aware of the fact that
the Smithian model of an 'early and rude' state of society fails
to cope with cooperation and joint labour (as Hodgskin himself
had noticed when he had tried to use it as a model for an alternative society where the whole product of labour belongs to the
labourer). Thompson, however, considers 'market failure' to be
a much more general phenomenon than Hodgskin does. The
existence of profits and the deviation of 'social prices' from
'natural prices' is explained by the fact that market exchanges
are necessarily crippled by fraud and unequal exchanges, giving
rise to profits. From the latter point of view, Thompson is opposed
to Hodgskin. The author of *Labour Rewarded* considers the
higgling of the market as necessarily bringing about unjust
exchanges and remuneration, while the author of *Labour Defended*
considers the higgling of the market as the only certain just rule,
which, unfortunately, is not always possible to apply. Furthermore, 'social regulations' are, according to Hodgskin, the cause
of the deviation from the 'just' natural prices to the unjust social
prices. Thompson holds the opposite view and notices how only
very complicated social regulations could implement a scale of
'just' but unequal remuneration.

As in point of fact the remuneration of labour, or wages
representing it, is nowhere regulated by calculations of
difficulty, hardship, unhealthiness, strength, skill, utility or
mental effort as compared with muscular or good disposition
(inclination to industry) of the labour; but by a variety of

accidents and chances, comprises in the phrase 'proportion of supply to demand' and entirely independent of regular connection with any of these circumstances; how, if we wish to alter this chance mode of remuneration and to substitute some fancied just, but unequal mode of apportioning to every different species of labour, its appropriate reward, shall we set about this most difficult operation? First we must lay down our principles of remuneration, next we must discover the means of applying these principles to the individual worker. (Hodgskin, 1827, p. 33)

Thompson believes that neither of these operations is feasible. As to principles, in what proportions should we reward good disposition, skill, mental as compared with muscular exertion, etc? (p. 33). A rule cannot be worked out. Moreover, he notes that, even if the 'scale of remuneration for every species of labour were made out', this scale would not last for very long. 'The skill, the capacity for hard or repulsive operations, even the utility of one year, might be as they frequently have been, utterly useless the succeeding year' (p. 44).

As to the applying of these 'varying principles to every individual worker', Thompson observes that the situation is no less desperate. 'An inquest must be held on every labourer in the country. Who are to be the inquisitors? How often is the inquisition to be renewed to keep pace with the moral and physical changes of the labourers?' (p. 35). Thus he reaches the conclusion that the higgling of the market gives an unjust scale of remuneration because people are allowed to speculate and profit from exchange, but that any attempt to 'reform' the scale of remuneration given by the market would bring about insurmountable difficulties. This reinforces his claim that 'equal rewards' are the only feasible solution for distributing income in a society where the whole product of labour belongs to the labourer.

The latter solution is also preferred on moral grounds, as we have already seen. Although Thompson sharply departs from the 'early state' socialism of Hodgskin, he shares with him the understanding of the enormous complications that the non-homogeneity of labour involves for stating a rule concerning the distribution of the product under socialism. His awareness of these complications, rather than a lack of insight into them, leads him to propose a system of remuneration that is actually unrelated to the kind of work performed. Thompson believes that exertion and coordination of labour can be achieved independently of remuneration differentials. He never, however, mentions that, under a rule of equal rewards, the inequality of the species of labour performed might be as unjust as the inequality of rewards for the same species of labour.

3.4 Bray and Gray

The Ricardian belief that it is possible to estimate labour in time units suggests an easy, even if erroneous, solution to Gray and Bray, who can be properly called 'Ricardian socialists' at least from this point of view. Gray moves from the proposal for a cooperativistic society outlined in his books, *A Lecture on Human Happiness* (1825) and *The Social System* (1831), to a simple monetary reform proposed in his book, *Lectures on Money* (1848). The idea that it is possible to estimate values objectively is probably taken by Gray not only from the Ricardian school but also from Robert Owen, with whom Gray had been collaborating in Lanark.

'The average physical power of men', Owen had maintained, 'has been calculated and the average human labour can be ascertained; and as it forms the essence of all wealth, its value in every article of produce may also be ascertained and its exchangeable value with all others fixed accordingly' (Owen, 1970, pp. 207–8). This belief suggests to Gray that exchanges can be made 'equal', and exploitation ended, simply by reforming the market system. A bank may issue notes to the workers in exchange for the value that the products of the workers embody in terms of time units. The latter system has the additional advantage of avoiding the economic crisis that can arise from unequal exchanges.

In J. Bray's *Labour's Wrongs and Labour's Remedy* (1839), however, we find the most complete description of a socialist society which is based on a system of equal exchanges and rigorous implementation of the labour theory of value. Bray justifies the assumption of the homogeneity of labour in the following way:

> Labour is neither more or less than labour; and one kind of employment is not more honourable or dishonourable than another, although all descriptions of labour may not appear of equal value to society at large. Such inequality of value, however, is no argument for inequality of rewards; and when we have examined the subject in all its bearings and relations, we shall find that it is as just and reasonable that equal labour of all kinds should be equally remunerated as it is

just and reasonable that labour should be universal. Man
properly constituted, requires not the low stimulant of
superior pecuniary reward to spur him on to do his duty to
his fellow-man. (Bray, 1839, p. 44)

Like Ricardo, Bray however, does recognize one element of
non-homogeneity in labour arising from the fact that different
units of labour may embody different amounts of training time.
For this reason he maintains that 'Under the present social system,
with its individualized and opposing interests, and its high and
low employments, equal remuneration for equal labour would
be both impracticable and unjust' (1839, p. 45). On the contrary,
'Under a rational system of communion and cooperation, where
society at large would take upon itself the education and employment of all its members ... equal remunerations would be as just
towards the inventor of a steam-engine as towards the maker of
the engine, or the man who sets it in motion' (p. 46). He maintains
that 'Men work not for labour's sake, but for wealth's sake; and
that all labour must ever be directed as to procure increased
wealth or increased leisure' (p. 183), that 'that system which
enables men to produce and appropriate the greatest quantity
of wealth with the least expenditure of labour will be the best
system, if its transactions be governed by the just principle of
equality of exchanges' (p. 179). The system that fulfils these
conditions is, according to Bray, a system of communities that
specialize in different activities and exchanges according to just
prices equal to the labour that is embodied in the goods exchanged.
The optimal size and the specialization of the communities allow
the achievement of production efficiency, while exchanges
performed according to the labour theory of value assure justice
and a direct link between production and consumption, which
avoids the possibility of a crisis.

3.5 Conclusion

In conclusion, the starting point of the debate in the 1820s and
1830s can be considered to be Hodgskin's observation that a socialist
society cannot rely completely on the market mechanism for solving its coordination and distribution problems. The necessity of
cooperation and joint labour is the cause of Hodgskin's departure
from a model of socialism that would otherwise resemble very
closely the 'early and rude state' of society described by Smith.
While Hodgskin shares with the latter the theory of value and the

conception of labour, he does not fall into the Smithian mistake of considering market exchange as the only, or even a sufficient, means for organizing the division of labour among society's members. He is, however, unable to provide an alternative rule for organizing production and distribution. The criticism of the market as a means of organizing a future society is extended and accentuated by Thompson, who advocates an egalitarian distribution and believes that the exertion and coordination of the labours of society's members can be achieved independently of remuneration differentials. Unlike Hodgskin, he does not understand that market exchanges, in spite of fraud and inequalities, play an important role in coordinating the decisions of society's members.

Bray and Gray deserve the name 'Ricardian socialists' in the same way in which Hodgskin and, with some caution, Thompson could be called 'Smithian socialists'. If the starting point of the latter economists is a 'model of socialism' that recalls the early Smithian state, Gray and Bray derive their concept of socialism from a characteristic feature of the Ricardian school: the idea that labour can be objectively measured and defined and that, consequently, values can be expressed in terms of 'homogeneous human motion'. If 'labour-values' can be objectively estimated, they can also be determined independently of those 'market exchanges' that cause 'exploitation' and unjust profits. Unjust profits are due to the fact that market values are not equal to the 'natural values' of commodities, the latter being equal to the quantity of labour necessary for producing them. For this reason, Bray and Gray propose to calculate values according to the labour expended in production.

The contribution of Bray and Gray anticipates the results of Wieser, Pareto and Barone, who will maintain that value is not necessarily a market phenomenon, and can be calculated, at least in theory, independently of actual market exchange (see chapters 5 and 8). There are, however, two serious limitations to the Ricardian socialists' approach. The first stems from the fact that values that are calculated according to labour-time expended in production are not necessarily equilibrium values. The fact that a commodity requires a certain amount of labour-time in order to be produced does not imply that society's members will be willing to pay a proportional value for obtaining it. The commodity might have been produced using an 'inefficient' technique, so that members would prefer to buy the same commodity from people who had used less labour-time for producing it. Moreover, even excluding the latter problem, there may be an insufficient demand for a certain labour-value of the commodity, for the simple reason that consumers desire a lower amount of that commodity at that value.

The second limitation of the Ricardian socialist approach derives from the Ricardian assumption that labour is homogeneous. Bray excludes the fact that different types of labour can be desired or undesired in very different ways by society's members. He assumes that the latter only desire consumption goods and are actually indifferent towards the allocation of their labour-power. These very restrictive assumptions are almost identical to the assumptions that Mill makes when he analyses the criteria according to which labour should be divided among society's members. We have already seen how such assumptions can only lead to Mill's conclusions. According to the latter, Babbage's principle is not only accepted, but should be extended from the firm to the whole of society. The analysis of these two limitations will be the starting point of the contribution of Karl Marx and Friedrich Engels, which we are going to examine in the next chapter.

3
Single-firm socialism and anti-firm communism

Introduction

We have seen in the preceding chapter that the approach of the Ricardian socialists is seriously handicapped by two limitations. First, they do not realize that their system of 'just exchanges' on the market fails to provide a coordinating mechanism for the economic system. Second, their pricing criterion is based on the restrictive and unjustified assumption that labour is homogeneous.

The first section of this chapter examines Marx's and Engel's contribution to the solution of the first problem. They observe that coordinating mechanisms other than the market can be used under socialism, and that these mechanisms are found even under capitalism. In their model of socialism the coordination of economic decisions relies on planning, which – they observe – is already used within the capitalist firm. Their model of early socialism is an extension of firm-type coordination to the whole economy – which is therefore transformed into a single-firm economy. Only within such an economy can the 'just transactions' envisaged by the Ricardian socialists be realized, and the labour theory of value applied as a pricing and, more generally, a planning tool.

Section 2 examines the contribution of Marx and Engels to overcoming the second limitation of the Ricardian socialists. Marx and Engels maintain that the assumption of homogeneous labour is not in general justifiable as a characteristic defining labour. On the other hand, they consider such an assumption a good approximation to the reality of some actual economic systems. Under capitalism, the profit-maximizing employer introduces a division of labour such that labour becomes a homogeneous pain. Such a situation would still exist in the early stages of socialism – implying that the labour theory of value, which also relies on the assumption of homogeneous labour, can be used as a planning tool in these circumstances. The goal of a socialist society is still to increase social wealth and not yet to change the nature of labour.

Although the model of early socialism can be considered as a single-firm society, the final goal of a communist society presents quite opposite priorities to those of the profit-maximizing firm. The goal of communism is the introduction of a new division of labour and a new organization of production such that labour becomes an enjoyable activity.

The final section underlines some weak or even contradictory points which make the Marxian analysis a rather ambiguous instrument of social change. While some of these points are related to a certain undervaluation of the market, a fundamental weakness of the Marxian approach concerns the belief of Marx and Engels that 'single-firm socialism' could smoothly transform itself into 'anti-firm communism'.

1   The single-firm model

1.1   Marx's critique of the Ricardian socialists

The theory of exploitation used by Ricardian socialists was based on the discrepancy between natural values (labour-embodied values) and actual market values. This theory had an enormous impact on their theory of socialism, for they believed that an institutional change was required to bring about just exchange, i.e., exchanges that would not give rise to unjust profits.

The Marxian theory of exploitation is completely different. It is built upon the assumption that we are in an equilibrium situation where commodities are exchanged according to labour-embodied values. In the Marxian theory of value, exploitation occurs because labour-power is exchanged according to the quantity of labour embodied in it (i.e., the amount of labour that is necessary to produce labour-power. Capitalists realize a profit in the Marxian theory of value precisely because they buy labour-power *at its natural value*.

The quantity of labour-time that is embodied in labour-power is, according to Marx, less than the actual time for which labour-power can be employed in production. And for this reason, capitalists buying labour-power at its natural value can realize a profit.

Exchanges according to labour-embodied values are not incompatible with Marx's theory of exploitation. According to Marx, however, two conditions must be satisfied for values to be proportional to embodied labour under capitalism. First, we must be in an equilibrium situation where demand equals supply. Second, each producer must employ his labour-time with 'average efficiency'; in Marxian terms, the labour employed by each producer must be the labour-time that is socially necessary for producing the commodity. Since according to Marx the Utopian 'equal market exchanges' of the Ricardian socialists belong to the actual world of capitalism, Marx is able to use his analysis of the actual market economy for criticizing them.

Recall that the Ricardian socialists used the labour theory of value as a tool for pricing commodities in a just society and maintained that a society could be efficiently coordinated by exchanging commodities at those values. Marx observes that, in a market economy, prices can be equal to the costs of production (or labour-embodied values) only when this coordination has already been achieved and demand equals supply. This is achieved by the market mechanism through the oscillations of market prices. An excess demand (supply) causes the market price of a product to be higher (lower) than its production costs. The difference between the market price and the production cost of a commodity induces producers to increase (decrease) production. This tends to decrease (increase) the initial excess demand (supply) and to decrease (increase) the market price. Such an adjustment process continues until demand equals supply and the market price is equal to the cost of production. The initial difference between the natural value (i.e., production cost) and market value of a commodity is therefore *necessary* to the achievement of the equilibrium of demand and supply, and is not the *cause* of their initial disequilibrium. On the contrary, the latter is the cause of the initial difference between natural value and market value.

The Ricardian socialists confuse the cause with the effect and maintain that fixing prices at their natural level will make demand equal to supply.

Marx criticizes Proudhon, who, he says, was simply re-proposing the thesis of the Ricardian socialists, in the following way.

Everyone knows that when supply and demand are evenly balanced, the relative value of any product is accurately determined by the quantity of labour embodied in it; that is to say, that this relative value expresses the proportional relation precisely in the sense we have just attached to it. M. Proudhon inverts the order of things. Begin, he says, by measuring the relative value of a product by the quantity of labour embodied in it, and supply and demand will infallibly balance one another. Production will correspond to consumption, the product will always be exchangeable. Its current price will express exactly its true value. Instead of saying like everyone else: when the weather is fine, a lot of people are seen going out for a walk, M. Proudhon makes his people go out for a walk in order to be able to ensure them fine weather. (Marx, 1955, p. 66)

The Ricardian socialists, by fixing market prices at their natural level, not only will not realize the equilibrium of demand and supply but also will prevent the achievement of such an equilibrium. The working of the market mechanism requires that disequilibrium be signalled by a difference between natural values and market values. While the market system will induce producers to supply those commodities that satisfy a certain social want, members of a Ricardian socialist type of society will have no inducement to produce commodities that are actually needed since they will be able to sell the latter anyway at their labour-embodied value.

We have seen that, according to Marx, equilibrium between demand and supply is not the only condition that must be satisfied in order for values to be proportional to embodied labour in a market economy. The quantity of labour embodied in a commodity should also be the labour-time that is 'socially necessary' for its production. 'The labour-time socially necessary is that required to produce an article under the normal conditions of production, and with the average degree of skill and intensity at that time' (Marx, 1967, vol. I, p. 39).

If values are fixed, according to the proposals of the Ricardian socialists, so as to be proportional to the labour-time that each producer has actually employed, and not according to the socially necessary labour-time, then, quite paradoxically, 'the more idle and unskillful the labourer, the more valuable would his commodity be because more time would be required for its production' (1967, vol. I, p. 39).

Such a paradox is avoided in the market economy by the fact that, 'by the mere effect of competition ... each producer is obliged to sell his commodity at its market price' – the latter being equal to the labour-time that is socially necessary for producing the commodity (1967, vol. I, p. 345). By obliging each producer who employs more than the socially necessary labour-time to produce a commodity to incur a loss, a certain kind of discipline is enforced by competition in the market system.

But under the Ricardian socialist system of equal exchanges, each producer is allowed to sell his product at a price equal to the quantity of labour that he has actually employed, and no authority will guarantee that producers have not wasted their time. The result, Marx maintains, will be a 'competition in idleness' (1955, p. 85).

In conclusion, any attempt to enforce market exchanges to occur at embodied-labour values is inevitably condemned not only to a theoretical, but also to a more dramatic practical, failure. Marx tried to prevent other socialists from applying these principles.

> Mr Bray's theory, like all theories, has found supporters who have allowed themselves to be deluded by appearances. Equitable-labour-exchange bazaars have been set up in London, Sheffield, Leeds and many other towns in England. These bazaars have all ended in scandalous failures after having absorbed considerable capital. The taste for them has gone for ever. You are warned, Mr Proudhon. (Marx, 1955, p. 87)

In 1885 Engels added, in a footnote to the German edition of the *Poverty of Philosophy*, that 'It is known that Proudhon did not take this warning to heart. In 1849 he himself made an attempt with a new Exchange Bank in Paris. The bank, however, failed before it had got going properly; a court case against Proudhon had to serve to cover its collapse' (Marx, 1955, p. 88).

1.2   *The division of labour and the firm*

We have seen in chapter 1 that a serious theoretical weakness of Smith's analysis of the division of labour was that he considered the market to be the only coordinating mechanism by which the division of labour could be organized. This limitation prevented him from having a full understanding of the factory system in spite of his celebrated pin-making example.

An enormous advantage of the Marxian approach is the full awareness of the fact that the market is not the only system by which the division of labour can be organized – or, indeed, was and is organized – in real economic systems.

> The division of labour is a necessary condition for the produc-
> tion of commodities (i.e., for products being exchanged on
> the market place), but it does not follow, conversely, that
> the production of commodities is a necessary condition for
> the division of labour. In the primitive Indian community
> there is a social division of labour, without production of
> commodities. Or, to take an example nearer home, in every
> factory the labour is divided according to a system, but
> this division is not brought about by the operatives
> mutually exchanging their individual products. (Marx, 1967,
> vol. I, p. 42)

Thus, while according to Smith market exchange is a necessary
condition for the division of labour, Marx maintains the opposite
point of view: the division of labour is a necessary condition for
market exchange, but the first can exist quite independently
of the latter (a clear example of the latter circumstance being
the factory). The capitalist economic system appears then to
Marx as a dual system in which two different coordinating systems
coexist, the first being the market and the second operating
within the factory.

Recalling Hodgskin's 'admirable work', Marx observes how
within the factory each individual labourer produces no commodity
that he/she can sell on the market (see Marx, 1967, vol. I, p. 355).
Thus, within the workshop, the division of labour is not brought
about by the purchase and sale of products but is organized by
the capitalist, to which several individuals have sold their labour-
power (i.e., their capacity for working). The capitalist will work
out a production plan such that definite numbers of workmen
are assigned to definite functions in the required proportions.

Marx contrasts the production plan that we have within the
workshop with the kind of coordination that is achieved by the
market outside it. While in the workshop the capitalist learns
the exact proportions according to which the different tasks have
to be performed, so that the 'iron law of proportionality' is applied,
in the market 'chance and caprice have full play in distributing
the producers and their means of production among the various
branches of industry.'

Of course, as we have already seen in the preceding section,
Marx is well aware of the fact that, even under the market system,
'the different spheres of production constantly tend to an
equilibrium' (1967, vol. I, p. 355). But Marx observes that this

adjustment process is very costly in terms of social resources because it is realized through economic crisis, bankruptcies, and an expensive *bellum omnium contra omnes*. A characteristic of the market system is the fact that decisions are first taken by the agents and only afterwards coordinated by the supply and demand mechanism. This implies that many producers may discover that the production decisions already taken are inconsistent with the satisfaction of social wants (i.e., they cannot sell their products at a price that covers their costs of production). It is true that the losses that the producers incur will bring about a tendency to reduce production and equate demand with supply. But this mechanism works precisely because some losses have been made and some social resources have been wasted. Moreover, as the market adjustment mechanism starts to work, new production decisions are taken the coordination of which is again realized through new imbalances of demand and supply and new losses. For this reason, Marx observes that under the market system the 'constant tendency to equilibrium of the various spheres of production is exercised only in the shape of a reaction against the constant upsetting of this equilibrium' (1967, vol. I, p. 356).

The market coordination of the division of labour is therefore characterized, according to Marx, mainly by its *a posteriori* nature, by which he means that there is tendency to coordinate production decisions only after they have been implemented. In other words, the correction of every mistake can only involve great losses of social resources.

Marx contrasts the *a posteriori* nature of market coordination with the *a priori* system by which the division of labour is organized within the workshop. Under the latter system the capitalists first coordinate the activities of the workmen in a production plan and then afterwards implement the plan; that is, within the firm the equilibrium between demand and supply is first achieved on paper in a production plan, and only afterwards carried out by the producers.

The conscious *a priori* coordination of the division of labour within the factory can therefore be contrasted with the unconscious coordination of the market process – the first kind of coordination having the great advantage of saving the resources that are lost during the long and costly market adjustment. The two systems are different because the sequence of implementation and coordination of production decision is reversed, and also because of a different kind of authority required. Under the market system the producers of commodities 'acknowledge no other authority but that of competition, of the coercion exerted by the pressure of their mutual interests' (1967, vol. I, p. 356).

We have already seen how the 'authority of competition' ensures that the work of the producers is expended only in the production of those commodities that satisfy a 'social want', and that only the work that is socially necessary for producing certain commodities is actually remunerated; on the contrary, 'the division of labour within the workshop implies the undisputed authority of the capitalist over men, that are but parts of a mechanism which belongs to him' (1967, vol. I, p. 356). The 'authority of the capitalist' replaces, within the factory, 'the authority of competition'. In the workshop the fact that a certain job satisfies a social need is assured by making each worker act within the framework of a production plan; according to this plan, each worker is ordered to do a certain kind and amount of work only when such work is useful.

It is the orders of the capitalist (and not the losses or the gains that he may incur when trying to sell the product) that constrain the worker to perform an activity that is required by society. The authority of the capitalist also replaces a second function of competition, by paying each worker according to the time that is 'socially necessary' for producing a certain commodity. Whenever the worker is idle or inefficient the capitalist can apply sanctions against him by lowering his pay or even firing him.

According to Marx and Engels, the capitalist economy is not only characterized by a dual coordination system of which the market is only one part, but also exhibits an increasing tendency to replace market-type coordination by firm-type coordination. The fact that within the firm the costly movements of demand and supply are replaced by the cheaper production plan of the capitalist is an important reason why firm coordination can replace the market system in coordinating certain spheres of production.

Moreover, Marx underlines the advantages and even the necessity of cooperation or joint labour which Gioia had already described. The latter can be advantageously exploited within a firm in a way impossible for a set of independent producers of commodities. Furthermore, independent producers cannot enjoy the advantages of applying a detailed division of labour to the production of a commodity – advantages that had been celebrated by the many economists referring to the high productivity of the pin-making factory. Finally, Marx observes how the exploitation of modern machinery requires large-scale production, which is possible only within big firms. The advantages of scale explain why a process of concentration takes place in the economy; the self-employed producers of commodities and small firms find it increasingly difficult to compete with larger firms, which then take over their business and hence become even bigger.

Within the institutional framework of capitalism, then, the market is not the only coordinating system and, moreover, the coordination of the economy takes place increasingly in the planning offices of the large firms.

1.3   *The early socialism model*

In his *Poverty of Philosophy*, Marx observes that

> Society as a whole has this in common with the interior of a workshop, that it too has its division of labour. If one took as a model the division of labour in a modern workshop, in order to apply it to a whole society, the society best organized for the production of wealth would undoubtedly be that which had a single chief employer, distributing tasks to the different members of the community according to a previously fixed rule. But this is by no means the case. While inside the modern workshop the division of labour is meticulously regulated by the authority of the employer, modern society has no other rule, no other authority for the distribution of labour than free competition. (Marx, 1955, p. 151)

The Marxian model of socialism can be considered as 'the society best organized for the production of wealth', which is mentioned in the above passage. In this model not only is the division of labour in the workshop organized according to a plan, but a 'chief employer' (the socialist state) organizes the distribution of work among the different spheres of production. Under socialism the authority of the 'chief employer' is extended from the workshop to society as a whole, replacing completely the 'capricious authority' of competition. Socialism can therefore be considered a single-firm society in which a single plan coordinates production. From this point of view it completes that process of concentration of production decisions which, according to Marx and Engels, capitalism has already started by allowing the growth of few big firms.

The advantages of cooperation, large-scale production and non-market *a priori* coordination (i.e., planning), which can already be seen at work under capitalism, will be completely exploited only under socialism. Moreover, under socialism the benefits generated by these advantages will not be appropriated by a small minority but will contribute to the wealth of the whole society.

The introduction of a coordination system other than the market allows Marx to conceive of a social system in which everyone receives – after some deductions have been made by the state for administration costs, education, health, etc. – 'exactly what he gives to it' (Marx, 1978, p. 32). The individual gives to society 'his individual quantum of labour'. He receives back 'a certificate from society that he has furnished such and such an amount of labour' (after the deductions mentioned above), 'and with this certificate he draws from the social stock of means of consumption as much as costs the same amount of labour'. Marx can conclude that under socialism the same amount of labour that an individual gives to society 'in one form he receives back in another' (p. 32). Recall now that the idea of 'a just exchange' of equal values, each expressing the same amount of work, had been the basis of the model of socialism of Gray, Bray and Proudhon, and that the latter had been criticized as a theoretical and practical failure by Marx. What then makes it possible for Marx's model of socialism to have that 'exchange of equal values' that was bound to fail in the Utopian world of the Ricardian socialists? It is precisely the fact that in the Marxian model this 'equal exchange' is realized not through the market, but by extending some of the characteristics of firm-type coordination to the whole of society.

In the market system 'equal exchanges' can occur only in an ideal, theoretical situation in which demand equals supply. Enforcing 'equal exchanges' in actual situations where demand does not equal supply makes it impossible for the market system to coordinate economic decisions. In the Marxian model of socialism 'equal exchanges' are possible because the equilibrium between demand and supply is not dependent on the market system but is realized through the conscious intervention of a 'chief employer' (i.e., a central planning office), who allocates labour to those kinds of production that satisfy social wants. Moreover, under the market system, fixing prices in such a way that they are equal to the actual time that each producer has taken to produce them brings about not the 'equal exchanges of equal labour time' that had been envisaged by the Ricardian socialists, but rather 'a competition of idleness'. In the Marxian model of socialism 'equal exchanges of equal labour time' are possible because the 'authority of competition' has not been rendered inactive without finding an alternative form of authority. The authority of the 'chief employer' and his assistants (i.e., the socialist state) takes the place of the 'authority of competition'. The state can check that each firm is employing the amount of time that is socially necessary for producing a certain commodity. If a firm is employing more than the time that is socially necessary, the state can apply towards that firm the same means of pressure that is applied towards the workers within the workshop under capitalism. Marx has a ready reply for those who may argue that the authority of the socialist state would violate their freedom of action:

> The same bourgeois mind which praises division of labour in the workshop, life-long annexation of the labour to a partial operation, and his complete subjection to capital as being an organization of labour that increases its productiveness – that same bourgeois mind denounces with equal vigour every conscious attempt to socially control and regulate the process of production, as an inroad upon such sacred things as the rights of property, freedom and unrestricted play of the individual capitalist. It is very characteristic that the enthusiastic apologists of the factory system have nothing more damning to urge against a general organization of the labour of society, than that it would turn all society into one immense factory. (Marx, 1967, vol. I, p. 356)

1.4   *Socialism and labour values*

On the one hand, Marx criticizes the idea of the Ricardian socialists that the market could be reformed by enforcing 'equal exchanges' at prices fixed according to the labour theory of value. On the other hand, he develops the intuition of the latter according to which values could be determined independently of exchange and used for distributing products among the members of the society. In other words, he specifies the conditions that are required in order for the labour theory of value to be applied as a pricing tool; these are essentially the adoption of planning and the authority of the socialist state.

Marx stresses the independence of value from actual exchanges on the market by using the very common example of the Robinson Crusoe one-man economy. He observes that the relations between Crusoe and the objects that he produces 'contain all that is essential to the determination of value' (1967, vol. I, p. 77), and he maintains that necessity itself compels Crusoe 'to apportion his time accurately between his different kinds of work'. 'Whether one kind occupies a greater space in his general activity than another, depends on the difficulties, greater or less, to be overcome in attaining the useful effect aimed at' (pp. 76–7). Marx imagines that Crusoe, 'having rescued a watch, ledger, and pen and ink from the wreck, commences like a true born Briton, to keep a set of books. His stock book contains a list of the objects of utility that belong to him, of the operations necessary for their production; and lastly, of the labour-time that definite quantities of those objects have, on the average cost him' (p. 77).

Thus, labour-time values can be calculated independently of exchange, since by definition it is clear that, in the Crusoe single-agent economy, no exchange occurs. On the other hand, the Crusoe economy can be considered as an extreme simplification of a planned economy. Marx observes that, in the case of a socialist society, 'in which the labour-power of all the different individuals is consciously applied as the combined labour power of the community, ... all the characteristics of Robinson's labour are here repeated, but with this difference, that they are social, instead of individual' (p. 78).

Labour-time values, which are only implicit in the Robinson Crusoe economy, can be usefully used in the case of the socialist society. On the one hand, they can be used to maintain 'the proper proportion' between a certain social want and the different kinds of work to be done to satisfy that want (p. 79). For example, if the community desires 10 pairs of shoes and the labour-time value of each one of the latter is 2 hours, we know that 20 hours of labour-time are necessary to satisfy that want (assuming constant returns to scale). On the other hand, by measuring the labour-time value of each product and the contribution to labour-time of each worker, we can distribute the products among the members of the community. For instance, if a worker has worked for 6 hours he is entitled to have 3 pairs of shoes.

In conclusion, while the Ricardian socialists had already had the intuition that values could be calculated independently of exchange, Marx had the merit of specifying the institutional framework under which this intuition could usefully be applied. Such an institutional framework was not a kind of 'reformed market economy', as the Ricardian socialists thought, but rather implied an extension of the non-market type of coordination from the firm to the whole economy.

2   *The anti-firm model*

2.1   *Introduction*

We have seen how the labour theory of value relies on the assumption that labour can be treated as a homogeneous quantity. While Ricardo had already noticed that labour could be reduced to homogeneous quantities as far as the difference in skills were concerned, he did not consider another major source of non-homogeneity of labour – that arising from the fact that the members of society derived different (dis)utility from the different activities that they could perform (see section 2.2 of chapter 2).

This problem, the importance of which had already been so well emphasized by Smith (see section 2.1 of chapter 2), has a crucial relevance not only if the labour theory of value is to provide a reliable explanation of exchange relations under capitalism, but also if it is to be applied as a pricing tool under a socialist economic regime. If different kinds of employment imply different (dis)utility, labour-embodied values cannot be market equilibrium values; the latter should allow lower wages for the more enjoyable forms of employment and lower values for the corresponding commodities being produced. On the other hand, when this source of non-homogeneity of labour-time is considered, the application of the labour theory of value as a pricing tool under socialism becomes indefensible. 'Equal exchanges' of labour time between each individual and society as a whole do not take into account the fact that these exchanges are very unequal when we consider the different disutility of the different types of employment of labour-time. In this case labour-time becomes an empty standard of measurement which does not express the social cost of the different activities. This circumstance becomes very clear when we recall that, according to Smith, (dis)utility was even *necessary* for establishing which human activities should be considered as labour. He maintained that hunting and fishing should be considered as 'amusements' in the advanced state of society while they were 'work' in its primitive stage, the change in definitions depending on changes in the technology and tastes that characterize these two stages (see section 2.1 of chapter 2). The planning office of a socialist society, which does not take into account the (dis)utility of the different types of employment, could therefore include among the social costs even activities that are an 'amusement' of that society's members. Apparently, equal exchanges of labour-time between individuals and society could in fact be as unequal as the exchange of a unit of time that gives disutility with a unit of time that is a source of enjoyment.

In general, Marx shares Adam Smith's point of view. His model of advanced communism – that is, of the society that should be realized after the model of socialism that was examined in the preceding section – is based on the idea that labour could become 'not only a means of life but life's prime want' (Marx, 1978, p. 34). However, he also maintains that the Ricardian assumption that labour-time could be considered as an homogeneous cost for society is not only justifiable but even rather useful when we consider capitalist society or the first stage of a socialist society.

We shall now proceed to examine the reasons why, according to Marx, labour can be considered an homogeneous source of disutility under capitalism and, therefore, in the first stage of socialism. The implications of this argument are that the labour theory of value is not handicapped by the non-homogeneity of labour either in explaining exchange relations under capitalism or as a pricing tool in the first stage of a socialist society. Section 2.3 then considers the Marxian model of 'advanced communism' which takes full account of his belief that labour is a source of (dis)utility.

2.2   Profit maximization and homogeneous labour

Marx maintains that the homogeneity of labour is a reasonable assumption under capitalism because of the way in which production is organized under this social arrangement. The distinguishing characteristic of capitalism lies in the nature of the employment contract. Marx considers this a peculiar market transaction in which labour-power is exchanged for a wage. 'By labour-power or capacity for labour is to be understood the aggregate of those mental and physical capabilities existing in a human being, which he exercises whenever he produces a use-value of any description' (Marx, 1967, vol. I, p. 167).

Thus, as a consequence of the employment contract, the employer acquires the right to use 'the capacity for labour' of the employee for a certain length of time. Although the employer 'buys labour-power in order to use it and labour power in use is labour itself' (p. 177), labour *per se* is not the object of a market transaction. While labour-power (i.e., the capacity for work) is exchanged on the market and its allocation among different firms is coordinated by the market mechanism, the *use* of labour-power (i.e., labour itself), which is carried out within the firm, is coordinated by the employer who has bought it and whose authority has been accepted by the employee as a consequence of the employment contract. The importance of this contract, within the Marxian framework, can be better appreciated when we consider that it defines the 'boundary' between the two coordinating systems – the market and the firm – which as we have seen in the preceding section characterizes the Marxian conception of capitalism. Up to the point at which the employment contract is signed, the employer and the employee are two agents of the market economy, the future employer being a potential buyer and the future employee being a potential seller of labour power. But after the signature of the employment contract, firm-type coordination replaces the coordination of the market.

It follows from this definition of the employment contract that the workers' preferences do not have any relevance in determining the characteristics of the labour process within the firm – that process (and therefore the homogeneous or non-homogeneous character of the labour being performed) is decided only by the employers. How do the employers organize the labour process?

Marx's analysis of the latter is one of the more interesting parts of *Capital*. Here we will limit considerably his exposition by simply observing that he shares the main aspects of the analysis of Babbage and Ure (see sections 2.2 and 2.3 of chapter 1). Since the capitalists (or Babbage's 'master-manufacturer') are interested in maximizing their profits, they will try to reduce labour-power costs per unit of product. This is achieved by introducing an extremely detailed division of labour in which the large majority of the workers perform only one simple task (cf. section 2.3 of chapter 2). The detailed division of labour *makes* labour an homogeneous quantity since the jobs being performed are reduced to similar simple movements among which it is unlikely that workers can have any preference.

'In the automatic workshop,' Marx observes, 'one worker's labour is scarcely distinguishable in any way from another worker's labour: workers can only be distinguished from another by the length of time they take for their work'. 'In short,' he adds, 'if there is a difference of quality in the labour of different workers, it is at most a quality of the last kind, which is far from being a distinctive speciality' (1955, p. 59). The homogeneity of labour is therefore a theoretical abstraction which is justified by the fact that it corresponds to a real characteristic of the capitalist economy. In his 'Introduction to the "Critique of Political Economy"' (1968), Marx underlines the real basis of this theoretical abstraction by maintaining that

> The indifference to the particular kind of labour corresponds to a form of society in which individuals pass with ease from one kind of work to another, which makes it immaterial to them what particular kind of work may fall to their share. Labour has become here, not only categorically but really, a means of creating wealth in general and is no longer grown together with the individual in one particular destination. (Marx, 1968, p. 44)

The labour theory of value, which relies on the assumption that workers are indifferent as between different allocations of their labour power, can therefore be used to explain exchange relationships under capitalism. It can also be used as a pricing tool during the first stage of a communist-planned society, whose characteristics we have examined in the preceding section; 'a communist society not as it has developed on its own foundations, but on the contrary, just as it emerges from capitalist society' (1978, p. 32). The same reasons for which homogeneous labour can be assumed to be a 'realistic abstraction' under capitalism can therefore be used to justify the use of labour theory of value as a planning tool under socialism. In the first stage of socialism 'the enslaving subordination of the individual to the division of labour and therewith also the anthesis between mental and physical labour' (p. 34) has not yet vanished. Labour is therefore still an almost homogeneous pain. At the same time, the aim of society is still to produce the maximum amount of wealth and is not yet to change the character of the labour process in such a way that labour can become an enjoyable activity.

2.3   Communism v. profit maximization

James Mill maintained that a society that aimed to maximize its welfare should adopt the same very detailed division of labour that, according to Babbage, is realized within the firm by the 'master-manufacturer'.

Recall that Mill had deduced this proposition from the assumption that the consumption of wealth was the only source of utility and, therefore, that labour could be treated as homogeneous human motion. We can summarize Mill's way of reasoning in the following way.

$$\text{(F1)} \quad \text{Homogeneous labour} \xrightarrow{\text{(D)}} \begin{array}{l} \text{An extremely detailed} \\ \text{division of labour should} \\ \text{be introduced in any society} \end{array}$$

We can now contrast the role of homogeneous labour in Marx and Mill. While the Mill uses the assumption of homogeneous labour to deduce that an extremely detailed division of labour should be introduced in any economic system, Marx deduces the realism of the assumption of homogeneous labour under capitalism from the fact that under capitalism employers introduce a very detailed division of labour. According to Marx, the theoretical abstraction of homogeneous labour can be justified only by referring to a specific situation where a detailed division of labour has already been applied; by contrast, according to Mill, labour is 'naturally' homogeneous (i.e., it can be assumed to be homogeneous under any economic system). We can summarize Marx's way of reasoning in the following way:

$$\text{(F2)} \quad \begin{array}{l} \text{Profit-} \\ \text{maximizing} \\ \text{behaviour} \\ \text{of the} \\ \text{employers} \end{array} \xrightarrow{\text{(A)}} \begin{array}{l} \text{An} \\ \text{extremely} \\ \text{detailed} \\ \text{division} \\ \text{of labour} \end{array} \xrightarrow{\text{(B)}} \begin{array}{l} \text{Indifference} \\ \text{to the} \\ \text{particular} \\ \text{type of} \\ \text{employment} \end{array} \xrightarrow{\text{(C)}} \begin{array}{l} \text{Homo-} \\ \text{geneous} \\ \text{labour} \end{array}$$

It is clear that, if we accept Marx's starting point, Mill's proposition becomes an empty statement which is based on circular reasoning. We can immediately see that if, starting from (F2), we join (F2) and (F1) we obtain

$$\text{(F3)} \quad \xrightarrow{\text{(A)}} \begin{array}{l} \text{An extremely} \\ \text{detailed} \\ \text{division} \\ \text{of labour} \end{array} \xrightarrow{\text{(B)}} \xrightarrow{\text{(C)}} \xrightarrow{\text{(D)}} \begin{array}{l} \text{An extremely detailed} \\ \text{division of labour} \\ \text{should be introduced} \\ \text{in any society} \end{array}$$

From the Marxian point of view, Mill is simply maintaining that a detailed division of labour should be introduced on the basis of the assumption of homogeneous labour, the validity of which requires that a detailed division of labour is introduced. From the Marxian point of view, Mill's conclusion is therefore incorrect since it involves circular reasoning.

On the other hand, if we assume that a detailed division of labour has already been introduced, Mill's line of reasoning can be used to show that certain social choices can be conditioned by a certain type of organization of society. A detailed division of labour could serve to encourage in the members of a society what Marx would call the 'false consciousness', and what we could also call the 'informational constraint', that work is necessarily a homogeneous source of disutility under any social system. The social system would make them believe that only an even more detailed division of labour could increase social welfare by increasing the amount of useful output being produced. The detailed division of labour and the 'false consciousness' would reinforce each other in these circumstances. The 'informational constraint' would bring about what Marx would call 'a product fetishism'.[1]

Quite paradoxically, members of society would accept that the aim of maximizing the output being produced should shape their social relations of productions; while the social relations of productions would not be affected by the very obvious circumstances that the activities of the members of society – including the time during which they are employed in production – is an important source of (dis)utility. Thus, while members of society would give great importance to the things being produced, they would treat their own manpower as a thing to the allocation of which they are completely indifferent. Marx's model of a communist society is based on a critique of this 'product fetishism'.

The definition of 'political economy' itself, as the term had been given by Mill and was accepted by many economists, was affected by product fetishism: Mill had maintained that political economy was concerned with the study of the ways by which society, conceived as one large family, could supply as many products as possible, consumption of products being the only aim of society. It followed from such a definition that the dictum of political economy was that society should organize itself according to the same criteria that Babbage's 'master-manufacturer' would use in organizing his firm (see section 2.3 of chapter 2). In particular, any alternative society to capitalism should have followed the same criterion. By contrast, Marx believes that his single-firm model of socialism can evolve into an advanced communist society where the division of labour is organized according to criteria that are very different from the criteria of the Babbage's firm.

From his 'Economic and Philosophical Manuscripts' onwards, Marx's writings contain a critique of such a definition of the aims of political economy. In this early work Marx observed that, for Ricardo, 'Nations are merely workshops for production' and 'men are nothing, the product everything' (1975, p. 306). He criticized the approach of political economy by pointing out that the fact that labour 'is harmful and destructive' depends on the fact that 'its goal is restricted to the increase of wealth' (p. 288).

And this restricted goal implied that there was no inconsistency between the goals of the profit-maximizing employer and the goals of the members of society as far as the organization of production was concerned. There could have been (and for some political economists there was) a goal incongruence and a social conflict about the distribution of the product, but it was certainly in the interest of all members of society – both employers and employees – that production should be organized in such a way that the output of the latter was as great as possible. A profit-maximizing employer would certainly have tried to achieve an organization of production and division of labour that would maximize the amount of output being produced by a certain amount of labour-power. Greater production was tantamount to more profits and to an increase of wealth, which was the only goal of society. The belief that goal incongruence between employer and employee was limited to the sphere of the distribution of the product is aptly summarized in the following account that Marx gives of the approach of political economy.

> Production yields goods adopted to our needs; distribution distributes them according to social laws; exchange distributes further what has already been distributed, according to individual wants; finally in consumption the product drops out of the social movement, becoming the direct object of the individual want which it serves and satisfies in use. (Marx, 1968, p. 27)

In this scheme, where 'production appears as the starting point' and 'consumption as the final end', 'Production is determined – according to the political economists – by universal natural laws, while distribution depends on social chance' (1968, p. 28).

But if we accept the Marxian observation that the goal that the political economists had attributed to society and to their science is too restrictive, the interests of the profit-maximizing employer and those of the other members of society may well diverge. Social conflict is then no longer limited to the distribution of the product but can arise in the context of the organization of the production and the division of labour. While the employer chooses the latter in such a way that the output obtained by employing a certain amount of manpower is as great as possible, the employees are interested in an organization of production such that they also derive more satisfaction (or less dissatisfaction) from their work. Production is not organized according to 'universal laws' within the firm under capitalism; it is shaped by the particular interests of the employers of labour-power, who take into account only the goal of increasing the product, and not the other goal of society, namely the increase of the level of satisfaction that workers derive from their labour.

The political economists considerably restrict the set of the possible goals of society by including in them only the improvement of those activities that involve the consumption of useful goods. Marx is not only persuaded that an improvement of the *quality* of those activities that involve the production of useful goods could be achieved under a different social system, but he also believes that under communism labour could become the most important source of satisfaction. According to Marx, the satisfaction that is derived from the activities of production lies mainly in the fact that we are able to realize something that we have ideated – a distinctive human capacity.[2]

The profit-maximizing employer does not allow its workers to use their capacity of ideation. Cost minimization requires the application of the Babbage principle, which implies that the activities of ideation should be performed by few individuals; the great majority of the workers merely execute what their managers have decided. In this way the training costs that would be incurred in order to make them able to use their ideation capacities are saved. Moreover, their managers will apply the Babbage principle to decisions about the structuring of their jobs and will dictate that the task each worker has to perform will be as repetitive and simple as possible; in this way a further saving of training cost is achieved.

The goals of a communist society stand in sharp contrast with the goals of the profit-maximizing employer. While the latter does not care that an improvement of the quality of the time expended at work can improve the welfare of the society, the Marxian communist society takes full account of the fact that the welfare of its members depends on the quality of the whole set of activities that they perform. The division of labour is therefore arranged in a completely different way under a system of advanced communism. The activity of production that any member of society performs no longer entails the boring execution of a very narrow set of tasks; everyone performs production activities in which his/her ideation and fantasy are used, activities that are made interesting and various. Everyone carries out a share of mental and a share of physical activity, avoiding the crippling effects of performing only one type of activity. Under a regime of advanced communism, Marx therefore maintains, labour is not only a 'means of life' as it is considered to be by the employee of the profit-maximizing firm, but also 'life's prime want' (1978, p. 34).

While Marx believed that the model of socialism considered in the preceding section could evolve smoothly into the model of advanced communism, the contrast between these two models is striking. The first extends some features of the internal organization of the firm, such as planning and the authority of the (chief) employer to the whole society. The division of labour that takes place in the firm is not challenged and is rather applied to the whole society. As in the case of the profit-maximizing firm, the goal of society is to maximize the amount of output being produced, and homogeneous painful labour still exists so that the labour theory of value can still be used as a planning tool.

By contrast, the model of advanced communism emerges in antithesis to the organization of production of the firm. The contrast between the goals of the private firm and the goals of a communist society is as great as the contrast between the restrictive goals that traditional political economy had assigned to society and the much wider goals that Marx believed human society could finally achieve. The main goal of communism is to remove the pain from labour. Consistent with his pain-theory of value, Marx limits the application of the labour theory of value to the first stage of socialist society. According to him, labour-time and labour-values will have ceased to play any role in a communist society. (On this point see section 3 of chapter 4.)

3   Marx v. Marx

The understanding that (1) society can be coordinated by means other than the market and (2) the division of labour can be organized according to criteria different from those of the profit-maximizing firms can be considered as the two great contributions of Marx and Engels to the economic theory of socialism.

While the preceding sections of this chapter have illustrated the importance of these two achievements, the aim of this section is to underline some weak or even contradictory points which make the Marxian analysis a rather ambiguous instrument of social change.

One weak point in the Marxian analysis lies in the fact that, while the social costs of using the market mechanism are stressed, the costs of using firm-type or planning coordination are almost ignored. It is true that Marx observes that an increasing number of managers, bureaucrats and supervisors has to be used in the larger firms under capitalism; this is a typical cost of using firm-type coordination. However, he does not perceive that, since these costs are unlikely to decrease too much under socialist planning, they should be compared with the costs of using the market in order for the issue of planning-versus-market to be correctly stated. While Marx correctly underlines that market and planning coexist under capitalism, he comes to the extreme conclusion that the market should not exist at all under socialism. This conclusion arises from an undervaluation of some relative advantages of the market.

This bias of Marx against the market is even more evident in his ignorance of the Smithian and Hodgskinian argument that the market takes into account the preferences of the workers in the allocation of their own manpower (see sections 2.1 and 3.2 of chapter 2). According to Smith, market values taken into account the relative (dis)utility of the different employments since workers agree to work for a lower wage in those employments yielding a lower disutility. An employer who offers worse working conditions is 'constrained' by the market to pay a higher wage, or he will lose his workers.

Now it is true that Marx has good reasons for believing that this 'market constraint' is very weak – largely because of the nature of the employment contract, which gives the employers the authority of organizing the production process, and because of the existence of unemployment, which makes particularly costly the 'exit' from unsatisfactory jobs.[3] This 'market constraint' cannot, however, be completely ignored.

In Marx's single-firm socialism, such a constraint cannot operate because of the absence of a labour market. Moreover, according to Marx, the only criterion according to which the division of labour should be organized under socialism is still the production of the maximum amount of wealth. We have seen how this criterion is equivalent to the profit-maximization criterion, as far as the choice of the organization of production and of the division of labour are concerned (see section 2.3 of chapter 2). It follows that, whatever the negative aspects of the organization of production and division of labour of the firm under capitalism, they are likely to be even more pronounced under the Marxian model of socialism, since in the latter case the single firm operating in the economy is not even facing a market constraint; workers cannot move to another firm if they are not satisfied with their working conditions.

In spite of the fact that the workers' preferences seem to be completely neglected under his single-firm socialism, Marx seems to believe that this organization of society can smoothly evolve into his model of advanced communism. There, these preferences are taken into full account and labour becomes an enjoyable activity. His line of reasoning seems to be as follows. The increase of wealth that is realized under the single-firm model of socialism will allow members of society to perform the productive activities they like, and in the way in they like, under advanced communism.[4]

There is certainly some truth in the fact that an increased stock of capital goods, and an increased productivity of labour, can allow members of society to have more time to dedicate themselves to enjoyable activities. However, it can also happen that the accumulation of wealth itself becomes an endless purpose of the society. The output produced by society may continuously increase while the welfare of the society may even decrease because less enjoyable productive activities are being performed.

In other words, there is no reason to believe that Marx's single-firm socialism should automatically evolve into his model of advanced communism. On the contrary, there are some reasons for believing that Marx's single-firm socialism is even more likely to be a victim of product fetishism (see n. 1) than a society in which the market constrains the decisions of the employers concerning the organization of the labour process.

Even if, under socialism, the socialist managers do not earn profits, they may be still interested in the fact that the goal of society is only the maximization of the output being produced. Such a social goal justifies their allocative power over labour, since their authority can be respected for the fact that they 'objectively' decide which allocation of manpower maximizes output. By contrast, the belief that the preferences of society concerning the allocation of manpower should also matter would challenge their authority and would necessarily mean that all the members of society should have a say in the allocation of manpower and the division of labour being adopted.

The socialist managers would not be the only members of society who may be interested in diffusing such a type of 'product fetishism'. We have seen that Marx believed that the profit-maximization behaviour of employers has made labour homogeneous under capitalism. This is because workers can be assumed to be indifferent among jobs that have been emptied of any skill content and hence are very similar to each other. However, the application of the Babbage principle instead creates a hierarchy of jobs characterized by different levels of skill requirements, and the assumption of homogeneous labour is likely to be a good approximation only for jobs at the bottom of the hierarchy. Only the latter jobs may be empty of any skill content, and hence it can be assumed that workers are indifferent only to them.

By contrast, preferences among the jobs at the higher levels of the hierarchy, and between them and bottom-level jobs, are very likely to exist not only under capitalism, but also under socialism. Therefore members of society who perform the top-level jobs may be interested, even under socialism, in the diffusion of product fetishism, as it justifies a division of labour under which they are allocated the more interesting and enjoyable jobs. Taking into explicit account the preferences of society about the allocation of manpower may challenge the character of objective necessity in the division of labour decided by the socialist managers.

Although an examination of the Marxian materialistic conception of history is beyond the aim of this book, it may be worth noticing that the Marxian faith in the automatic transformation of early socialism into advanced communism is strictly related to some weak aspects of this conception, according to which the development of the productive forces is the ultimate cause of the change of the social relations of production. In our case, the development of productive forces that is achieved under socialism, should change the relations of production of the latter society into the relations of production of advanced communism.

If the evolutionary link between single-firm socialism and a society that I call 'anti-firm communism' (because of the contrast of its objectives with those of the profit-maximizing firm) is rejected, then the Marxian project of transformation of society becomes rather ambiguous. The two Marxian models lose the unity implied by their presentation as two steps of a single project. 'Being Marxist' itself becomes a very ambiguous statement. On the one hand, it can mean being in favour of the extension to the whole society of the authoritarian and hierarchical world of the profit-maximizing firm. On the other hand, it can mean sharing the Marxian criticism of the organization of production and division of labour that takes place in the profit-maximizing firm, and favouring a new way of organizing production – in particular, one that takes account of the needs of the members of society not only as 'consumers' but also as 'producers'.

Notes

1 In *Capital* (1967, vol. I. ch. 1) Marx uses the term 'commodity fetishism'. He indicates by this term two different phenomena. The first indicates the failure to understand that values are not intrinsic qualities of things but are quantities embodied in them and an outcome of market relations. The second arises when the particular kind of labour (i.e., homogeneous-abstract labour) that is the source of the labour-embodied values is confused with the activity of production in general. According to Marx, the activity of production assumes the form of homogeneous-abstract labour only under particular real circumstances such as the ones examined above. This second phenomenon of fetishism indicates the failure to understand that the homogeneous-abstract character of labour under capitalism is not an intrinsic quality of the activity of production. I call this second aspect of fetishism 'product fetishism'. It indicates the failure to understand that in general the activity of production could be very non-homogeneous and that society therefore should care not only about the bundle of goods produced but also about the quality of the various employments of labour. I prefer using the term 'product fetishism' instead of 'commodity fetishism' because I believe that 'product fetishism' can characterize also societies in which products are not commodities as in Marxian single-firm socialism. This last point will be treated in the third section of this chapter.

2 See Marx (1967, vol. I, p. 178), where he maintains that 'what distinguishes the worst architect from the worst of the bees is this, that the architect raises his structure in imagination before he erects it in reality.'

3 These two points are related. The employers have the authority to organize the production process only if the 'exit' from the firm is costly for the workers. In the Marxian framework the existence of the 'reserve

army of labour' makes 'exit' particularly costly; in a situation where unemployment exists, the authority of the employer can be very strong because under these circumstances either the 'cost' of quitting a job or the 'cost' of being fired from a job can be very high. On this point see the last section of chapter 9 and, in particular, n. 6, which shows that the incompatibility between capitalism (in particular, the authority of the employer) and full employment can be 'translated' into the language of modern mainstream economics.

4   Marx (1978, p. 34) postpones the advent of communism until 'after the productive forces have also increased with the all-round development of the individual and all the springs of cooperative wealth flow more abundantly'.

4

Value, communism and the definition of labour

Introduction

In the first section of this chapter a simple model of inter-dependence of human activities is put forward. A society chooses to perform some activities, and some other activities have to be performed in order for the chosen activities to be carried out. Labour is endogenously defined as the deficit of necessary activities (i.e., is the difference, for each activity, between the amount of activity that has been chosen and the amount that it is necessary to perform). This model allows a distinction between the Marxian model of communism, in which labour defined as a deficit level of necessary activity has disappeared, and other types of society.

In section 2 two different specifications of this model, obtained under two different assumptions, are examined. The first is based on the restrictive assumption that society chooses to perform only the activities of consumption, and that the activities of production are never chosen as an end in themselves. In this case the concept of labour as a deficit of necessary activity becomes equivalent to the concept of labour as the activity of production of consumption goods. The second specification is based on the more general assumption that any activity, including the activities of production, could be chosen as an end in itself by society. In this case the two concepts of labour outlined above are no longer equivalent. The approaches of Marx and the Ricardian school are compared. While the Ricardian school model is based on an exogenous separation of means and ends and a restrictive assumption of homogeneous labour, the Marxian model is shown not to be based on these two limitations. Using these two specifications of our model, the issue of the transition from the Marxian model of early socialism to communism is re-examined.

In the final section the Ricardian and Marxian theories of value are compared and it is argued that there is an important qualitative difference between these two theories, which is related to a different definition of the kind of labour that is a source of value. Finally, Marx's standpoint, which implies that the law of value cannot hold under his model of advanced communism, is examined.

1   *A model of human activities*

We denote by $X_1, \ldots, X_m$ levels of any kind of human activity and by $\bar{X}_i$ the level of activity i that a society has chosen to perform. $\bar{X}_i$ is therefore called the 'chosen level of activity i'.

Furthermore, we assume that the amount of activity X_i that is required in order to carry out the activity X for a standard unit of measure is given. For instance, one hour of scientific research might require five minutes to clean the laboratory, eight minutes to set up the equipment that is used during the experiment, and so on. We call these ratios of interdependence among activities 'activity coefficients'. An activity coefficient b_{ij} therefore indicates the amount of activity i that is necessary in order to guarantee one standard unit of the activity j.

Our matrix of activity coefficients is as follows:

$$\begin{matrix} b_{11} & \ldots & b_{1m} \\ \vdots & & \vdots \\ b_{m1} & \ldots & b_{mm} \end{matrix} = \mathbf{B}.$$

Given the matrix $\mathbf{B}$ of activity coefficients, it is possible to calculate the levels of activities $(X_1, \ldots, X_m)$ that are necessary in order to perform any given vector $[\bar{X}_1, \ldots, \bar{X}_m]$ of chosen activities. We call these levels 'the necessary levels of activity'.

In order for any chosen vector

$$\bar{\mathbf{X}} = [\bar{X}_1, \ldots, \bar{X}_m]'$$

to be carried out, every necessary level of activity X_i must satisfy the following condition:

$$X_i = b_{i1} \bar{X}_1 + b_{i2} \bar{X}_2 + \ldots + b_{im} \bar{X}_m \quad i = 1, \ldots, m \quad (1.1)$$

In words, the (total) level of each necessary activity i must equal the sum of the levels required in order for each one of the chosen activities to be performed.

(1.1) can be rewritten by using matrix notation as follows:

$$
\begin{array}{c}
X_1 \\
\vdots \\
X_m
\end{array}
=
\begin{array}{ccc}
b_{11} & \cdots & b_{1m} \\
\vdots & & \vdots \\
b_{m1} & \cdots & b_{mm}
\end{array}
\begin{array}{c}
\bar{X}_1 \\
\vdots \\
\bar{X}_m
\end{array}
\qquad (1.1')
$$

or, denoting by $\mathbf{X}$ the vector of the necessary activities,

$$\mathbf{X} = \mathbf{B}\bar{\mathbf{X}}. \qquad (1.1'')$$

Two alternative properties can characterize the solution of our model according to the actual values of the matrix $\mathbf{B}$ and the vector $\bar{\mathbf{X}}$:

(a) For every activity i the level of $\bar{X}_i$ that has been chosen by society is greater than or equal to the level X_i of this activity that is necessary in order for the chosen vector $\bar{\mathbf{X}}$ of activities to be performed; i.e.,

$$\forall\, i \in [1, \ldots, m] \quad X_i \leqslant \bar{X}_i. \qquad (1.2)$$

(b) For at least one activity i the level $\bar{X}_i$ that has been chosen by society is less than the level X_i of this activity that is necessary in order for the chosen vector of activities $\bar{\mathbf{X}}$ to be performed; i.e.,

$$\exists\, i \in [1, \ldots, m] \quad X_i > \bar{X}_i. \qquad (1.3)$$

It is clear that in this second case the members of society have to perform a deficit level of necessary activity. This is due to the fact that the necessary level of at least one activity exceeds the level that members of society have chosen to perform. For each activity i, we denote by D_i this deficit level of activity i, and we define D_i more precisely in the following manner:

$$D_i = \max\,(0,\, X_i - \bar{X}_i). \qquad (1.4)$$

We will also denote by $\mathbf{D}$ the (total) deficit of necessary activity, the latter being equal to the vector

$$[D_1, \ldots, D_m]'.$$

We can now use the concept of deficit of necessary activity for giving the following definition of labour.

Definition 1.1 For each activity i the deficit level of necessary activity is called labour. The (total) labour that is carried out by a society is therefore equal to the (total) deficit of necessary activity that is performed by the latter. If we denote by **L** the (total) labour performed by a society, then

$$\mathbf{L} = \mathbf{D} = [D_1, \ldots, D_m]'.$$

This definition of labour is consistent with the Smithian insight that, if labour is an activity that gives disutility (i.e., if the members of society do not choose spontaneously to perform it), then the particular activities that should be considered to be labour can be determined only endogenously on the basis of the technology (i.e., the matrix **B**) and the tastes of society (i.e., vector $\bar{\mathbf{X}}$). Only on the basis of these data is it possible to determine whether fishing or hunting, or only a part of one of these activities, should be considered as labour or as an amusement. (On this point chapter 6's section 2.1.)

Definition 1.1 is also consistent with the Marxian approach which distinguishes between labour as painful activity (which we call 'labour') and labour as an enjoyable activity of production. On the other hand, we keep the word 'labour' only for labour as a painful activity, while the 'enjoyable' activities of production are included among the chosen activities $\bar{X}$. This change in terminology is done merely to clarify the issue, and the argument that follows can be retranslated into the Marxian terminology. We can now give a Marxian interpretation of the two properties (a) and (b) which, as we have seen, can characterize the solution of our model.

A society for which the solution of our model is characterized by property (a) can be identified with the Marxian model of advanced communism. Under communism no deficit of necessary activity is performed, and therefore, because of definition 1.1, no painful labour has to be carried out. Of course, under communism certain activities are necessary in order that the enjoyable activities chosen by society can be performed, but the tastes and the technology of society are such that these necessary activities are themselves enjoyable and some members of society will choose to perform them.

Societies for which the solution of our model is characterized by property (b) face a quite different situation. If the chosen level of activities is to be performed, a deficit level of necessary activity has to be carried out for at least one of them. Because of definition 1.1, this is tantamount to saying that some (painful) labour has to be performed. The problem of the distribution of these deficit levels of necessary activity, or in other words the problem of the division of labour, arises in these societies.

The division of labour can be more or less inegalitarian. We can consider the extreme case of a slave society, in which one class performs all the chosen activities (which may include all 'non-consumption' activities, such as participating in the political life of the state-town, reading and writing books, etc.) and another class performs all the labour that is required in order for the chosen activities to be carried out.

On the other hand, we can consider a much less inegalitarian society, such as the Marxian model of early socialism. A distinguishing character of this society should be that it tends to eliminate the problem of the division of labour completely, or in other words tends to change itself into the model of advanced communism, which we have examined under (a).

2 Definitions of labour

The definition of labour given in the preceding section can now be compared with the definition of labour that is implicit in the Ricardian school framework.

The view of the production process that the Ricardian school had in mind can be usefully described with the help of a slightly generalized version of the Leontief model (see Pasinetti, 1977). Society chooses to consume a certain vector of goods $\mathbf{C}$, and in order for $\mathbf{C}$ to be produced, it is also necessary to produce all the direct and indirect inputs, which are equal to:

$$\mathbf{Q} = [\mathbf{I} - \mathbf{A}]^{-1}\mathbf{C}$$

where $[\mathbf{I} - \mathbf{A}]^{-1}$ is the Leontief inverse matrix.

Labour can be then *defined* as a vector $\mathbf{L}^*$ which is necessary to produce $\mathbf{Q}$. (Each component L_R^* of $\mathbf{L}^*$ denotes a particular type of labour employed in the production of $\mathbf{Q}$); i.e.,

$$\mathbf{L}^* = \mathbf{EQ}$$

where $\mathbf{E}$ is a matrix of labour input coefficients, and each element e_{RS} of $\mathbf{E}$ denotes the quantity of L_R^* that is required in order to produce a unit of Q_s (where Q_s denotes a component of the vector $\mathbf{Q}$). Since in the Ricardian framework labour is assumed to be homogeneous, it is possible to sum up the components of

L^* and to obtain the total amount of labour h required to produce Q; i.e.,

$$h = \sum_{R} L_R.$$

We can visualize our generalized version of the Leontief model in the following way:

$$C \xrightarrow{[I-A]^{-1}C} Q \xrightarrow{EQ} L^* \xrightarrow{\sum_{R} L_R^*} h.$$

We can also visualize the model considered in the preceding section in the following manner:

$$\bar{X} \xrightarrow{B\bar{X}} X \xrightarrow{X-\bar{X}} L. \tag{2.2}$$

If we make the following assumption, we can better understand the relationship between these two ways of looking at the economic system and defining labour.

Assumption 2.1   All the 'chosen activities' are consumption activities. The production of goods is never chosen as an end in itself and is an homogeneous activity.

When this assumption is accepted, we can consider (2.2) and (2.1) as two equivalent models assuming that C is a function

$$C = \alpha \bar{X}$$

of the chosen levels of activities.

Since we assume that no chosen activity involves the production of goods, it follows from assumption 2.1 that the necessary activities (which are required only in order to produce consumption goods) are never chosen activities. Whenever an activity is 'necessary', its chosen level is zero; i.e.,

$$\forall i \in [1, \ldots, m] \quad X_i > 0 \Rightarrow \bar{X}_i = 0.$$

A consequence of assumption 2.1 is therefore that, because of (1.4),

$$\forall i \in [1, \ldots, m] \quad D_i = X_i$$

which implies, because of definition 1.1,

$$X = L.$$

Moreover, assumption 2.1 implies that the necessary activities are only required in order for the consumption goods **C** to be produced, since under this assumption the performing of the chosen vector of activities **X̄** only requires the consumption of products. Then

$$X = L^*$$

since **L*** is exactly the levels of necessary activities required for the production of consumption goods **C**.

From assumption 2.1 it follows therefore that

$$L = X = L^*.$$

Moreover, since in assumption 2.1 it is also assumed that the production of goods is an homogeneous human activity, it is also possible to write

$$\sum_R L_R = \sum_R X_R = \sum_R L_R^* = h.$$

As a consequence, under this assumption the two models are equivalent and (2.1) and (2.2) can be unified in the following way:

$$\bar{X} \xrightarrow{\alpha \bar{X}} C \xrightarrow{[I-A]^{-1}C} Q \xrightarrow{EQ} L^* = X = L \xrightarrow{\sum_R} h. \tag{2.3}$$

In this expression the first three arrows embody the assumption of the separation between ends and means (the ends of society **X̄** do not overlap with the means, **L*** or **X** or **L**, that are necessary for achieving them), and the last arrow embodies the assumption that the activities that are the means for achieving the ends of society are homogeneous.

Thus, under assumption 2.1 the Ricardian way and the Marxian way of looking at the economic process coincide. The two definitions of labour (i.e., labour as a deficit of necessary activity and labour as the activities required for producing consumption goods) also coincide, because assumption 2.1 implies that the deficit of necessary activities is equal to the total level of necessary activity that is required in order for the consumption goods to be produced.

An important difference between the Marxian and Ricardian approaches, however, lies in the interpretation of the specification (2.3) of model (2.2) obtained under assumption 2.1.

With reference to Mill's definition of political economy (see chapter 2, section 2.3), expression (2.3) expresses the economic problem of any society. The only end of society is to consume a certain amount of goods, and labour is the homogeneous necessary 'toil and trouble' that is required in order for these goods to be produced.

Within the Marxian framework, (2.3) does not express the general formulation of the economic problem of any society. By contrast, it can be considered only as a description of the nature of the economic process of particular institutional frameworks. Examples of the latter are the capitalist and early socialist societies.

Under capitalism the production of commodities requires that homogeneous painful labour is performed within the profit-maximizing firm. The members of society work in the firm only because this activity allows them to perform activities outside the firm. The activities performed outside the firm can be called 'activities of consumption'; by this term is meant activities requiring the consumption of the commodities that are produced within the firm. When we accept this terminology (the limit of which is that it does not take into account the fact that the so-called 'activities of consumption' do often involve domestic labour), we can then say that 'consumption activities' are the only 'chosen activities' under capitalism, and that labour, defined as a deficit of necessary activity, equals the amount of necessary activity that is required for the production of consumption goods.

For the same reason, (2.3) can be considered a description of a Marxian model of early socialism where the activity of production, which is carried out within the single firm operating in the economy, is still in general painful. The only enjoyable chosen activities are still carried out outside the firm when the products of the firm are being consumed.

In spite of this similarity, it is important to recall that (2.3) has different interpretations under capitalism and under the Marxian model of socialism. Under the former it describes the market equilibrium conditions among the various sectors of production, while under the latter it describes the production plan of a socialist society.

While (2.3) can give an approximate description of actual institutional frameworks, however, from a Marxian point of view it cannot be considered a general description of the economic process of any society. The Marxian model of advanced communism examined in the preceding section is a strong counter-example to the alleged generality of the specification (2.3) of model (2.2). In general, Marx believes that production activities can become 'chosen activities' and be a source of enjoyment under the organization of production of the communist society. A more general specification of model (2.2) is required for a description of the Marxian model of communism, which is characterized by the fact that no activity of production can be considered as labour if the latter is defined as a deficit of necessary activity.

Assumption 2.2 The 'chosen activities' can be consumption activities *and/or* production activities. The production of goods *can* be chosen as an end in itself.

Assumption 2.1 is a particular case of assumption 2.2 and can be arrived at from assumption 2.2 by adding the restrictive condition that the production of goods can never be chosen as an end in itself and that the activities of production are homogeneous activities.

Under assumption 2.2, labour defined as a deficit of necessary activity and labour defined as the activities required for producing the consumption goods are, in general, two different vectors **L** and **L***. This is due to the fact that in this case not all the level of necessary activity **X** is necessarily a deficit of necessary activity. Since a part of it (or even all of it) can be chosen by members of society if they enjoy certain activities of production. Then:

$$0 \leqslant D_i = X_i - \bar{X}_i \leqslant X_i \quad i \in [1, \dots, m]$$

and

$$0 \leqslant \mathbf{L} \leqslant \mathbf{X} = \mathbf{L}^*.$$

Under assumption 2.2, model (2.2) can therefore be specified as follows:

$$\bar{\mathbf{X}} \xrightarrow{\alpha \bar{\mathbf{X}}} \mathbf{C} \xrightarrow{[\mathbf{I}-\mathbf{A}]^{-1}\mathbf{C}} \mathbf{Q} \xrightarrow{EQ} \mathbf{X} = \mathbf{L}^* \xrightarrow{\mathbf{X}-\bar{\mathbf{X}}} \mathbf{L}. \tag{2.4}$$

In this specification of model (2.2), the restrictive assumption that the activities that society wants to perform (the ends) never overlap with the activities required to perform them is not made. Moreover, the necessary activities are not assumed to be homogeneous. And we can see that in this more general formulation labour defined as a deficit of necessary activity does not any longer generally coincide with labour defined as the activities required for the production of the consumption goods.

Model (2.4) can clarify how, within the more general Marxian framework, since the activity of production **L*** is not identified with **L** (i.e., labour defined as a deficit of necessary activity), a communist society becomes a theoretical possibility which occurs in model (2.4) when

$$\bar{X} \geqslant X = L^*$$

and therefore

$$L = 0.$$

A characteristic of a Marxian communist society, therefore, is that the consumption goods are produced using only chosen activities and that no labour (i.e., no deficit of necessary activity) has to be performed.

The Ricardian socialists, who identified the activity of production with painful homogeneous labour and the activity of consumption as the only end of society, could only conceive socialist alternatives that were characterized by a fairer distribution of the consumption goods and of the labour performed. A model like model (2.3) was in their mind. By contrast, Marx had in his mind a model of the 'labour process' like (2.4). Such a model was equivalent to model (2.3) only under the restrictive assumption 2.1, which Marx identified with the actual characteristics of the capitalist society and early socialism. In general, the Marxian model could allow the conception of an alternative society characterized by an organization of production and a technology such that even the disappearance of labour could become possible. On the other hand, Marx maintained that the aim of a socialist society was still the production of wealth, and the activity of production could be still considered as painful homogeneous labour in this society. Only later under communism could the activity of production become an end in itself (see chapter 2, section 3).

While Marx provides an excellent critique (see section 2.3 of chapter 3) of the view of economists such as Mill (a formalization of whose view could be considered model (2.3)), he postpones the application of this critique to his model of advanced communism. The planning office of a socialist society still applies a model like model (2.3) for organizing the activities of society and does not take into account the needs of the members of society as producers.

An increase of wealth, which is the end of model (2.3), does not however necessarily imply that painful labour-time necessarily decreases, even in the long run. The accumulation of wealth considered as the only end of society could make the communist society even more remote if it implies that the deficit of necessary activities increases. If the final aim of a socialist society is to make all the activities (including the activities of production) enjoyable, the preferences of society about all these activities must be considered from the very beginning. A socialist society should pay the maximum attention to the fact that its members have preferences not only about the products that they consume but also about the activities they perform. A model like model (2.4) should therefore be used from the outset by a socialist society instead of model (2.3). In other words, the end of society should also be to increase the level of those activities of production that its members choose to perform. The choice of the techniques should be aimed at reducing the deficit of necessary activities (i.e., labour) and replacing it with enjoyable chosen activities. In this way, and not (only) by increasing the wealth being produced, could a socialist society evolve into the Marxian model of communism where labour disappears.

3 Marxian and Ricardian labour values

Marx and the Ricardian school share a very similar explanation of exchange relations under capitalism. They both maintain that, under this institutional framework in equilibrium, values are proportional to the amounts of labour embodied in the commodities. The Marxian and Ricardian theories are however very different. This difference depends on a different definition of labour which characterizes these two approaches.

According to Marx, a merit of Ricardo was his observation that values were proportional to the amount of labour that was embodied in the commodities. On the other hand, Marx criticizes Ricardo for failing to understand that only a particular *kind* of labour can be a source of value.[1] The labour that Marx believed to be a source of value can be identified with labour as a deficit of necessary activity defined in the preceding section.[2] Only labour as a deficit of necessary activity needs the external incentives of a wage for it to be performed, because of its painful nature. On the other hand, whenever the activity of production is enjoyable (when it is a chosen activity as well) it does not need any external incentive and is not a source of value.

We can now use a simplified version of our model in order to compare these two theories of value. We consider an economy where the production of only two goods ($i = 1, 2$) is required in order for the chosen activities to be performed. We call l_i the amount of labour (as a deficit of necessary activity) and $\bar{x}_i$ and x_i the amounts of chosen and necessary activity embodied (directly and indirectly) in the production of one unit of good i. Then

$$l_i = x_i - \bar{x}_i \qquad l_i \geqslant 0 \quad i = 1, 2.$$

If we denote by V_1 and V_2 the values of goods 1 and 2, we can express the Marxian theory of value as follows:

$$\frac{V_1}{V_2} = \frac{x_1 - \bar{x}_1}{x_2 - \bar{x}_2} = \frac{l_1}{l_2}. \tag{3.1}$$

On the other hand, we have seen that the Ricardian school identifies the total amount of necessary activity required for producing a good with labour. Denoting by l_i^* this amount of labour (in this case defined as activity of production), we can express the Ricardian theory of value as follows:

$$\frac{V_1^*}{V_2^*} = \frac{x_1}{x_2} = \frac{l_1^*}{l_2^*}. \tag{3.2}$$

Under assumption 2.1, these two theories of values are equivalent because this assumption implies that

$$x_i > 0 \Rightarrow \bar{x}_i = 0 \qquad i = 1, 2$$

and therefore

$$\frac{V_1}{V_2} = \frac{V_1^*}{V_2^*}.$$

However, we have already seen that Marx and the Ricardian school would give very different interpretations of assumption 2.1. According to the Ricardian school (including the Ricardian socialists), the activity of production can always be identified with labour. By contrast, according to Marx the identification of the activity of production with painful labour is justified only with reference to the particular institutional framework of capitalism (or early socialism). The difference between these two theories becomes very clear when we consider the case of the Marxian model of advanced communism, where

$$\bar{x}_i \geqslant x_i \qquad i = 1, 2$$

While in this case the Ricardian values (3.2) would stay unchanged, the Marxian values (3.1) disappear since, because of definition 1.1,

$$\bar{x}_i \geqslant x_i \Rightarrow l_i = 0 \Rightarrow V_i = 0 \quad i = 1, 2.$$

Marx's statement that the law of value does not hold under communism is therefore not only correct within the classical theory of value (which linked value with painful labour), but also can be considered a result of a more general approach to the theory of value, which does not necessarily link the activity of production with painful labour.

A different theory of value – as the opportunity cost theory of value, which we are going to examine in the next chapter – can challenge the statement that value should disappear under communism. But the two fundamental insights of Marx – (1) that the activities that are the 'ends' of society are not necessarily different from the activities that are the 'means' for achieving them; and (2) that the human activity of production is homogeneous only under a particular institutional framework – still constitute, in my view, an advantage of the Marxian approach over the large majority of the subsequent theories which we are going to examine in the following chapters.

Notes

1   Marx criticizes 'political economy', and in particular Ricardo, for the fact that 'it has never once asked the question why labour is represented by the value of its product and labour-time by the magnitude of that value' (1967, p. 80). And in a footnote to the page, he adds that labour as production of 'use values' is not a source of value: labour as a source of value is 'abstract human labour'. On the other hand, Marx stresses that 'abstract labour' is not only a theoretical abstraction but also a real abstraction which characterizes capitalist production. The theoretical abstraction that is implicit in the concept of labour as source of value is based on the real homogenously painful character of labour under capitalism. (On this last point see sections 2.2 and 2.3 of chapter 3.)

2   Marx considers this deficit of necessary activity to be homogeneously painful for the reasons examined in sections 2.2 and 2.3 of chapter 3. In this section we make the same assumption. The limits of this assumption have already been examined in section 3 of chapter 3.

5

Some Austro-English disputes on disutility and cost

Introduction

The marginalist revolution has been often called the subjectivist revolution. The meaning of the latter adjective is intended to encompass the concept that only with the advent of the marginalist revolution did the subjectivity of the individuals and their preferences become the starting point of economic analysis. On the other hand, all three main authors of the marginalist revolution considered the subjectivity of individuals when such individuals were consumers. In assessing the notion of the subjectivity of individuals as producers and workers, the approaches of Jevons, the founder of the English stream of the marginalist revolution, and Menger, the founder of the Austrian school, were probably as different as the approaches of Smith and the Ricardian school (see section 2 of chapter 2).

From this standpoint there is, in fact, a certain similarity between the approaches of Jevons and Smith. Jevons's subjectivist revolution is not limited to the consumer, and, as in the case of Smith, the preferences of individuals for their work are carefully taken into account. By contrast, from the same standpoint, certain aspects of the approach of Menger can recall certain characteristics of the Ricardian approach. The subjectivist revolution of Menger is limited to a subject conceived only as a consumer. Rather like Ricardo and Mill, Menger implicitly assumes that the members of society have no preferences for their work.

Given these two different starting points, it is hardly surprising that the exponents of the second generation of the marginalist schools had some 'celebrated disputes' about the role of disutility and cost in economic theory (see Robbins, 1930, p. 207). In spite

76

of the fact that the almost general acceptance of the Walrasian approach, which we will examine in the next chapter, has made many economists understate their importance, these disputes are very interesting. This chapter will concentrate on the disputes after two preliminary sections briefly outline the contributions of Jevons and Menger on this matter. The relationship between the classical concept of cost and the concept of opportunity cost, which is one of the crucial points of the dispute, will be examined in section 4 in relation to the problem of the role of cost and value in a communist society.

1 *Jevons*

'Repeated reflection and inquiry have led me to the somewhat novel opinion, that value depends entirely upon utility.' This famous statement of Jevons (1970, p. 77) can give the misleading impression that his book, *The Theory of Political Economy*, takes into account only the individual's preferences for consumption goods as the source of this utility.

By contrast, as Collison Black points out in his Introduction to *The Theory of Political Economy*, the unity of the book, which has been challenged by both Robbins and Stigler, is to be found in Jevons's explicit attempt 'to treat Economics as a Calculus of Pleasure and Pain' and to work out 'an application of Bentham's utilitarian philosophy to the economic problem'.[1] In Jevons's conception of the economic problem, the pleasure and the utility derived from consumption goods are just as important as the pain and the disutility identified with labour by Jevons.

According to Jevons, labour 'is any painful exertion of mind or body undergone partly or wholly with a view of a future good' (1970, p. 189). Adam Smith had pointed out that activities such as fishing or hunting could bring about a future good and at the same time be an amusement. Jevons is well aware of the fact that some activities 'may be both agreeable at the time and conductive to future good'. On the other hand, he observes that even these activities are agreeable only in a limited amount; so that they become labour (i.e., painful activity) if they are carried out beyond a certain level. Economics as 'a Calculus of Pleasure and Pain' needs to take labour into account only when the activity becomes painful effort, because only after this point does the problem of weighting the advantages and disadvantages of labour arise. 'For this reason,' Jevons maintains, 'we must measure labour by the amount of pain which attaches to it', even if this pain can be negative (i.e., pleasure) when a certain type of activity is performed for a certain limited amount of time (p. 189). According to Jevons, not only the subjective evaluation of the units of the same occupation but also the preferences that the individuals have for different occupations make labour extremely non-homogeneous. He points out that the large majority of the English labourers usually will not work so hard as production increases. Yet he maintains that this is not true for some occupations, where by contrast 'success of labour only excites to new exertions, the work itself being of an interesting and stimulating nature' (p. 198).

Jevons applies his subjective 'Calculus of Pleasure and Pain' to solve the problems of how much labour an independent worker performs and how he or she distributes his or her labour among various occupations. This problem also has a wider meaning for Jevons, because he believes that the results obtained from its solution 'are identical in general character with those which apply to a whole nation' (p. 199).

Jevons starts by examining the simple case in which labour can be allocated only in a single occupation (i.e., in the production of a single good), so that the only problem that arises is how much work the labourer will perform. Jevons believes that the amount of labour (i.e., pain) that is 'contained' in additional units of work-time is decreasing at the beginning, because work is usually more irksome at first 'than when the mind and the body are bent at work' (p. 191). This decrease of pain that at the beginning accompanies the increase of work exerted can bring about 'an excess of pleasure ... due to the exertion itself', even if this exertion is painful at the beginning (p. 191). However, after a while, additional units of work-time start bringing about increasing amounts of labour and then an aggregate balance of pain. In the meantime, additional amounts of goods being produced bring about decreasing increments of utility. When the pain of an additional unit of work becomes equal to the corresponding pleasure gained from an additional unit of product, the 'free labourer' ceases to work.

In this way the problem of stating how much labour an independent worker will perform is solved by Jevons by an application of his 'Calculus of Pleasure and Pain'. The problem of the distribution of manpower among different occupations is directly treated by Jevons as the problem of the distribution of labour – labour being defined, as mentioned above, as the aggregate balance of pain accompanying exertion, and therefore being measured in the same scale of the utility of the products. Jevons states that 'when labour is finally distributed we must have the increments of utility from several employments equal' (p. 199). If the increment of utility is greater in one employment than in another, it would be better for an individual or a nation to allocate more labour in the employment where the increment of utility is greater.

In this case, the total amount of labour performed must be such that labour is 'carried on until the increment of utility from any of the employments just balances the increment of pain'; in other words, it is such that the increment of utility derived from any employment is equal 'in amount of feeling to the increment of labour by which it is obtained' (p. 200). The statement that labour must be distributed in such a way that the increments of utility from several employments are equal is expressed by Jevons as follows:

$$\frac{du_1}{dx}\frac{dx}{dl_1} = \frac{du_2}{dy}\frac{dy}{dl_2} \tag{1.1}$$

where du_1/dx and du_2/dy are, respectively, the marginal utilities of the products x and y, and dx/dl_1 and dy/dl_2 are the marginal productivities of labour in the production of x and y (p. 199). However, this formulation can be misleading (Jevons himself has some doubts about it – see his foonote at p. 200) until it is pointed out that l_1 and l_2 are not amounts of labour in the prevailing meaning of this term but rather the (dis)utility derived from exertion (or work).[3] A formulation of Jevons's statement, in terms of work-time, should take into account the fact that he believed that work-time affected utility in each use not only indirectly (via the utility of the product) but also directly (via the (dis)utility of work-time, which he calls labour).

After having shown how an individual (or a nation) decides how much labour to perform and how to allocate it among different occupations, Jevons integrates his 'Theory of Labour' with his 'Theory of Exchange' and describes how producers can realize welfare gains by exchanging their products. He deduces from his Theory of Labour that the marginal utilities of the products must be inversely proportional to the marginal productivities of labour performed in their production; i.e.,

$$\frac{du_1/dx}{du_2/dy} = \frac{dy/dl_2}{dx/dl_1}.$$

According to Jevons, this expression also means that, for each producer, the marginal utilities of the products must be proportional to their marginal costs, since the ratio of the productiveness of labour is the reciprocal of the costs of production. On the other hand, Jevons takes from his Theory of Exchange the statement that individuals can realize welfare gains by exchanging commodities up to the point where their marginal utilities are proportional to their prices. Hence, each producer will also adjust the ratio of the marginal costs to the ratio of prices. This is done by adjusting the ratio of the marginal cost to the ratio of the marginal utilities of the products. Marginal costs are therefore only indirectly adjusted to prices via an equalization of them to marginal utilities of the products, which is carried out independently by each producer.

It is clear from the way in which Jevons integrates his Theory of Labour and his Theory of Exchange that the kind of society he has in mind is characterized by its possessing a market only for the products of labour and not for labour itself. Only in this situation can each producer perform the two simultaneous but independent operations described above: on the one hand, to allocate labour in such a way that the marginal utilities of the products equal their marginal costs; and, on the other hand, to exchange the products in such a way that their marginal utilities equal their prices.

As Collison Black has well pointed out in his Introduction to Jevons (1970, p. 25), in Jevons's theory, 'the problems of organisation of labour do not arise' and nothing recalling even the foundations of a theory of the firm exists in his book. There is no employment contract, and there is no employer who decides how labour should be allocated within the firm. By contrast, in Jevons's world of independent producers, the labourers are absolutely free to decide how much to work and how to employ their labour. From a certain point of view this is a deficiency of analysis. Like Smith, Jevons does not seem to be aware of the fact that the division of labour can be coordinated, and usually has been coordinated, by means of other than the market.

We can, however, try to give a different interpretation of this characteristic of the *Theory of Political Economy*. We have seen how Jevons's work was intended to be an application of Benthamian ethics to economic problems, and that for Jevons economics was the study of the organization of the economy that should develop from the Benthamian 'Calculus of Pleasure and Pain'. In this framework, labour is considered by Jevons as a 'subjective feeling'. Therefore only the 'subjects' (i.e., the workers) can decide how much to work, how to organize, and how to allocate their labour, for the very reason that they are the only ones who can know anything about their own subjective feelings. In this interpretation, the society that develops from Jevons's application of Bentham's ethics is therefore incompatible with at least some aspects of capitalism, and in particular with the employment contract. For this reason, no employee-employer relation (i.e., no firm) is seriously examined in *The Theory of Political Economy*.

This interpretation would also be supported by the fact that later on in his life, in his book *The State in Relation to Labour*, Jevons (1968) was to regard the employment contract as a very imperfect arrangement and to advocate the arbitration and conciliation of the state in labour disputes. In addition, he also considered 'the cooperation of workmen who form joint-stock companies for the carrying on of manufacturing or agricultural industry independently of large capitalists ... highly desirable as far as it can be carried out (Jevons, 1968, p. 143, 145).

2   Menger

'How can it be that institutions which serve the common welfare and are extremely significant for its development come into being without a common will directed towards establishing them?' In Menger's book, *Problems of Economics and Sociology* (1963, p. 146), published more than a decade after his fundamental contribution to the marginalist revolution, he was to consider this as the central question of theoretical economics.

Menger does not share with Hayek, a living exponent of the Austrian school founded by Menger himself, the unilateral and conservative view that the 'institutions which serve the common welfare' cannot come into being by acts of 'common will' and *must* come from the unintended consequences of the actions of the individuals.[4] Menger observes that 'social institutions can be introduced by agreement or legislation', and that 'moreover there is no doubt that the further development of such institutions takes place as a rule in the latter way in times of higher economic culture' (Menger, 1963, p. 153). On the other hand, the role that Menger gives to economic theory is mainly to answer the above question. The structure of his *Principles of Economics* could already clearly show this approach to economics.[5]

In the *Principles* (Menger, 1950), the existence of the institutions of money and exchange is explained by showing how individuals can found these institutions merely by following their desire to satisfy their needs. No use of 'common will is therefore necessary for the creation of these economic institutions'. The *Principles* are therefore characterized by a causal structure, the starting point of which are the needs of the individuals. These needs explain how each person can give a subjective value to each good. In turn, the existence of these subjective values explains how individuals create the institutions of exchange and market prices simply by following their desire to satisfy their needs as much as they can. The institution of exchange is created at the very moment in which two individuals, A and B, recognize that A owns certain quantities of a good x which have for him a smaller value than certain quantities of a good y, while B owns certain quantities of a good y which have for him a smaller value of a good x. When A and B understand that they face this situation, they also understand that each can increase his wealth (measured by his own subjective values) by exchanging certain quantities of the two goods at any price that is in between the two subjective values (Menger, 1950, chapter 4). The institution of money is also similarly created by individuals pursuing their own interest. They realize that the direct exchange of their own goods for goods that have for them a higher subjective value is often impossible, and that they can approach their end by first getting goods that are more marketable than the goods they own. According to Menger, the secret of the institution of money lies in this discovery that there are some goods that are more marketable and can therefore perform the role of money (Menger, 1950, chapter 8, section 1).

This causal structure of Menger's *Principles*, which makes the subjective values of individuals the starting point for the explanations of market prices and in general market relations, is also very evident within the theory of subjective value itself (Menger, 1950, chapter 3). Menger believed that the value of a certain quantity of a certain good is equal, for a certain individual, to the importance of the least important needs that are satisfied with that quantity, i.e., to the importance of the needs, the satisfaction of which would be sacrificed if that quantity were not available. This statement, which is very clear for those goods that satisfy human needs directly, is extended by Menger to include other goods. In his theory, goods are arranged according to their 'distance' from the needs of the subject, which are the cause of their value. The goods of first order are those that directly satisfy human needs; the goods of second order are those employed in the production of the goods of first order; the goods of third order are in turn defined as the goods employed in the production of the goods of the second order; and so on. In this way, the definition of the subjective value of a quantity of a good can be extended to the goods of an order higher than the first. This is done by simply observing that these goods are indirectly necessary to the satisfaction of human needs; and that the satisfaction of some needs should be sacrificed if any quantity of the means of production, directly or indirectly employed in the production of the first-order goods, were not available.

This causal structure of Menger's theory of value can be compared to the structure of a train. The locomotive of the train represents the needs of the subject, while the first car is occupied by the first-order goods which derive their value (motion) directly from these needs. The other cars are occupied by the higher-order goods which derive their value (motion), solely by indirect means, from the utility of the products. (Edgeworth, 1925, p. 23, uses the image of a train to describe the Austrian approach.)

A problem now arises in Menger's theory: into which car should we fit human labour? In his entire book, Menger treats labour as a good of an order superior to the first order. He believes that labour derives its utility from its employment in the production of goods of an inferior order. Unlike Jevons, Menger does not seem to understand a peculiar aspect of human labour; namely, the circumstance that, by the very fact of being performed by the subject whose needs we are concerned with, labour affects these needs also directly. In the train metaphor, human labour is a peculiar passenger which does not fit into Menger's rigid and causal scheme because it always occupies two cars: it is a passenger of the first car with the other first-order goods, and it occupies some other car as well. In other words, roughly speaking, the value of labour, defined as the importance of the needs that are satisfied or dissatisfied by its employment, is derived from two factors: the importance of the needs that are satisfied by the product of labour, and the importance of the needs that the subject satisfies or dissatisfies through the process of working. Only in a footnote does Menger seem to realize that human labour cannot be treated like any of the other superior-order goods (1950, p. 171, n. 34). He admits that labour is usually linked with disutility, but the only conclusion that he derives from this is that it implies that labour always has to be an economic good. By this he means that labour cannot be a free good whenever it is effectively employed. Then in the same footnote he states, quite contradictorily, that the greatest part of the occupations of labour are pleasurable. He deduces this in order to show that the value of labour is derived from the utility of its product and not from the disutility of labour.

In conclusion, Menger does not seem to understand the basic difference between labour and any other of his higher-order goods, such as iron. The individual can care about the allocation of iron; and iron is likely to have a value for him, but only in so far as he derives utility from the product obtained by employing this iron – otherwise he can well be indifferent to its allocation. The same is not true for labour; because the allocation of labour is the allocation of the subject himself, who may prefer certain employments to others.

We have seen how the subjectivity of individuals and their needs is the starting point of all Menger's analysis and, in particular, of his theory of value and economic institutions. However, the personality of Menger's individual is so disunited that he recalls very closely what psychiatrists define as a schizophrenic personality. On the one hand, he is well aware of his needs when these needs concern the objects that he consumes; and on the other hand, the same individual treats the allocation of himself in production as the allocation of any superior-order object. In addition, this individual is indifferent to the needs that can be satisfied or dissatisfied by different human activities of production. The contrast of this approach with that of Jevons, who we have seen to define labour directly as a subjective feeling, could not be more striking.

3   The disutility of labour controversy

Menger's *Principles* were translated into English only in 1950. For a long time his approach had only an indirect influence on the English world, mainly through the works of his disciples Böhn-Bawerk and Wieser.

The starting point of the 'celebrated disputes' (Robbins, 1930, p. 207) of the 1890s and 1900s on the ultimate nature of real costs can be considered to be the 1894 reviews by Edgeworth (1925 edn, pp. 22–32 and 59–63) of the English edition of Böhm-Bawerk's (1894) *Positive Theory of Capital* (see Böhm-Bawerk,

1959 edn), which contained an exposition of the theory of value largely inspired by Menger's *Principles*, and of *An Introduction of the Theory of Value, on the Lines of Menger, Wieser and Böhm-Bawerk* by William Smart (1892), an English follower of the Austrian approach. In these views, Edgeworth criticized the Austrians for ignoring the fact that economic equilibrium is determined not only by utility but also by 'disutility cost and sacrifice'. He pointed out that '[t]hese remarks relate particularly to that mode of sacrifice which labour constitutes' (Edgeworth, 1925 edn, p. 29). By contrast, Böhm-Bawerk seemed to be aware of the 'sacrifice involved in the formation of capital' (p. 29). Edgeworth claimed that in Böhm-Bawerk's book he 'read little about the mobility of labour seeking the position of minimum cost in the sense of effort and sacrifice; little about the equations of the net advantages of the different occupations' (pp. 29–30). Böhm-Bawerk did not admit that 'costs exert a causal influence on the price of products' (p. 28); these costs were due to the disutility of labour (and the sacrifice of abstinence), which, unlike Jevons, the Austrians ignored.

According to Edgeworth, the Austrians were therefore guilty of ignoring two fundamental, strictly related, economic principles, without the inclusion of which a theory of value could be only half-completed: on the one hand, they ignored the importance of the great law of costs; on the other hand, they did not understand the fundamental role of the disutility of labour in economic theory.

The discussion that followed Edgeworth's reviews was concerned with both these issues (called synthetically by Böhm-Bawerk the 'laws of disutility' and the 'law of costs': Böhm-Bawerk, 1959 edn, p. 32). We will start examining the discussion concerning the law of disutility in economic theory; the law of costs will be examined in the following section.

In his article 'The Ultimate Standard of Value', Böhm-Bawerk (1894a) defends the Mengerian approach, which almost ignores the preferences of the same subjects for their work on the basis of some institutional features. These features distinguish the capitalist economy from an economy of independent workers or a Robinson Crusoe economy. Böhm-Bawerk admits that in the latter cases, since the labourer is entirely free to determine the length of his working day, he will take into account both the utility of the product and the disutility of labour. In these circumstances, he 'will continue his labour to that quarter of an hour, the disutility of which will be exactly counterbalanced by the utility of the goods produced in this quarter of an hour' (1959 edn, p. 20). In this equilibrium, the analysis of Jevons is therefore accepted. The (subjective) value of the product (which is in this case equal to the wage or the value of labour) is equal to both its marginal utility and the marginal disutility of the labour employed in its production. Böhm-Bawerk asks himself (p. 20), 'What, in this case, are the factors that determine the value of the product?' and replies that '"utility" and "disutility" are here of equal importance' (p. 20). In this case he agrees with Marshall, who had maintained that, in the determination of value, 'utility and disutility or pleasure and pain work together like the two blades of a pair of shears' (p. 21). Böhm-Bawerk adds that this analysis can be easily extended to the case in which the independent labourers sell their products on the market and satisfy, with their work, the needs of other individuals. In this case, the equilibrium market price will be such that all 'who desire to purchase at that price would be satisfied and, at the same time, the price would afford sufficient identification for the pain endured by just the right number of workmen' (p. 22). In this case, also, utility and disutility can be considered to 'work together like the two blades of a pair of shears' (p. 21).

'Here, however,' Böhm-Bawerk declares, 'my English and American colleagues and myself must part company' (p. 22). He holds that this rule, which assigns to 'utility' a role as important as disutility, 'has no wider application than is justified by the assumption upon which it is based; namely, the assumption that the labourer is entirely free to determine how long he will continue his daily labour' (p. 23). Such an assumption, Böhm-Bawerk feels, is generally in contrast with 'the actual facts of our present industrial life', where 'the labourer is not free to determine the length of his working day' and 'the hours of labour are fixed more or less by custom or law' (p. 23).

Böhm-Bawerk admits that the disutility of labour can still have some partial effects. For instance, he admits that differences in the agreeableness or disagreeableness of the various occupations will tend to give rise to differences in the range of wages (pp. 24–6). However, he believes that the preferences of individuals for their work cannot have the same weight as the preferences of individuals for the products that they consume; while the latter can operate independently of any constraint, the operation of the former is constrained by some institutional elements in a modern economy.

Commenting on Böhm-Bawerk's article, Edgeworth (1925) points out that the opposition between himself and Böhm-Bawerk 'is slighter than may have been supposed' and that 'it appears to consist principally in a different estimate of quantities which do not admit exact measurement' (p. 59). Edgeworth admits that Jevons's analysis of the equilibrium of the independent workers cannot be extended to the employers of the firms because it is not generally open to workers to vary the amount of their work-day. However, Edgeworth believes (and Marshall in his *Principles* shows the same opinion[6]) that disutility can still be considered 'an ultimate standard of value' because other mechanisms are open to the workers in order for their preferences to have a weight on the achievement of the economic equilibrium (Edgeworth, 1925, p. 29). On the one hand, he believes that, as far as piecework prevails within the firm, the workers can still change the intensity of their work. On the other hand, he maintains that 'disutility may be regarded as an independent variable so far as it is open to the worker to change from an unpleasant occupation if not compensated for its unpleasantness' (p. 61).

The discussion between Edgeworth and Böhm-Bawerk allowed the two economists to find a common ground which differed from either Menger's or Jevons's approaches to the problem of the preferences of the workers for their own work. Unlike Menger, Böhm-Bawerk and Edgeworth agreed that, in the case of the independent worker or in the case of a Robinson Crusoe single-man economy, the preferences of individuals for their work do matter in the determination of the economic equilibrium and the equilibrium values. Moreover, unlike Jevons, both Böhm-Bawerk and Edgeworth ended up emphasizing, although in different tones, that the freedom of choice enjoyed by the independent worker regarding the use of his own manpower is seriously limited in the case of the worker employed in the firm.

Finally, we can observe how this conclusion embodies a difficulty for the approach of Menger. Menger intended to deduce the birth of economic institutions from the simple interactions of individuals pursuing their self-interest independently of the authority of any individual in particular. According to Böhm-Bawerk (and this point is not refuted by Edgeworth), the organization of the firm requires that some decisions (such as stating how much and with what intensity to work) be made that affect all the individuals working in the firm. These decisions cannot be made separately by each individual in pursuit of his own private interest; rather, they must be made by an authority and implemented by more than one individual, for the very reason that they concern how individuals, characterized by different interests and preferences, are going to cooperate. Cooperation itself requires individuals to agree on the amount of work to be done and on their working conditions. The authority that plans and enforces cooperation among workers can be the expression either of the 'common will' of the workers themselves or of a non-democratic unit. In any case, it seems very unlikely that the institution of the organization of work in a productive unit can be comparable to the institution of exchange only by dint of the simple inter-action of separate individuals pursuing their own self-interest. The institution of exchange may require only that different individuals hold different subjective evaluations of their goods; by contrast, cooperation requires either that some persons agree on a common evaluation of their needs as workers, or that some give up their subjective evaluations and accept the subjective evaluation of another individual.

In some ways, the dispute between Böhm-Bawerk and Edgeworth brings economic theory slightly closer to one of the fundamental Marxian insights which had got completely lost in the marginalist revolution: the fact that the market and the firm constitute two different alternative institutions by which the economic activities of the individuals can be coordinated. While the former can be treated almost entirely with reference to the economic agents separately pursuing their own interests, the latter is also based on the *ex ante* planning of an authority that coordinates the activities of the workers (cf. chapter 3 above, section 1.2).

4   *Cost, choice and communism*

We have seen at the beginning of the preceding section that the dispute between Edgeworth and Böhm-Bawerk started with Edgeworth's criticism that Böhm-Bawerk ignored the 'law of disutility' and the 'law of costs'. We have also seen how, according to Edgeworth, these two laws were actually unified in one law, being cost identified with disutility and pain. By contrast, Böhm-Bawerk held, in his article 'The Ultimate Standard of Value' (1894a), that the law of cost and law of disutility are two distinct laws based on two different mechanisms (see Böhm-

Bawerk, 1959, p. 32). He claimed that, while the 'law of disutility' required (in order for it to be completely operative) that the worker be free to decide the amount and the allocation of his work, the 'law of cost' was based on a different mechanism, which required that barriers to entry be absent and factors able to move freely in the economy. For this reason Böhm-Bawerk maintained that, on the one side, 'the law of disutility includes but a small part of the territory covered by the empirical law of cost, and on the other, it includes a certain portion of territory which is not covered by the law of cost' (1959, p. 32). In some cases the 'law of disutility' may apply and the law of cost may not, as in the case of a self-employed monopolist who is free to decide the length of the working day (p. 29). By contrast, Böhm-Bawerk adjudged that the law of cost has a much wider application and can hold independently of the fact that the law of disutility applies. In all the cases in which 'the commodities are reproducible at will, ... the normal value of commodities tends in the long run to be equal to the sum of their costs, *in the sense of the expenses of the producer*' (1894b, p. 719). Even if the wages paid by the producers neither correspond to the marginal disutility of labour nor vary with it, the value of the product will still vary with the wages paid.

The Austrian school did not therefore deny the importance of the law of cost but instead broke the link between the law of cost and the law of disutility. The Austrians gave a different interpretation of the word 'cost' itself by developing the theory of opportunity cost, which links cost with the utility of the products. This theory, accepted by Böhm-Bawerk, was developed mainly by F. von Wieser, to whose contribution we now turn.

Wieser's article, 'The Theory of Value' (1892), was intended to be 'a reply to Professor Macvane', who had criticized the Austrian school (and in particular Böhm-Bawerk, in his article 'Böhm-Bawerk on Value and Wages', 1890). Wieser does, however, explicitly point out that his polemic is directed not only against Professor Macvane, 'but above all against Ricardo, on whose economic conceptions he has based his argument' (Wieser, 1892, p. 24).

It will be remembered that Smith and Ricardo had both linked the existence of value with the fact that painful labour had to be performed in order for the useful commodities to be produced, even if we have seen that they had characterized this link in different ways (see chapter 2, section 2). Within this pain–cost theory of value, Marx could well limit the existence of value to societies where the activity of production was painful. And he could conceive of communism as a society without painful labour and therefore as a society in which products have no value (chapter 2, section 3). With good reasons, therefore, Wieser maintains that, according to Ricardo, 'in the long run the value of commodities is determined by the exertion which is saved owing to their existence' (1892, p. 25) and 'properly wealth is labour saved' (p. 26). In the classical conception, labour is the origin of value because it costs the expenditure of effort. By contrast, Wieser points out that 'It is not at all necessary to take into account the arduousness of the labour in order to explain its value' (p. 40). Each kind of labour, like any other means of production, has value in so far as its quantity is limited in relation to the needs that it can indirectly satisfy by producing useful commodities. Under these conditions, 'value would be accorded to labour even if it involved no expenditure of effort whatever' (p. 40). Wieser believed that each kind of labour is valued according to its availability in relationship to the needs that it can satisfy. Whenever a type of labour is scarce in relationship to these needs, it obtains a value independently of the fact that it is painful.

It is this limited availability of each type of labour (or any other resource), and not its disutility, that is the cause of the fact that the use of manpower or other resources does generally involve a cost for society. Society has a limited possession of certain resources in relation to its needs, and 'since each productive process diminishes this possession, it reduces utility – it costs exactly as much as the value which the material and labour would have produced if rationally applied' (p. 42).

In this way, Wieser develops the foundations of what is now known as the alternative-use or opportunity theory of cost; i.e., 'the philosophy of the cost phenomenon that may be expressed by the adage: What a thing really costs us is the sacrifice of utility of those other things which we could have had from the resources that went into the one we did produce' (Schumpeter, 1954, p. 917).

We can easily see that this opportunity cost occurs quite independently of the disutility of labour. We can consider two activities A and B, both enjoyable, and assume that activity A is used for producing good X and activity B is used in the production of good B. If our time is limited, there is a cost of performing each one of these activities. For instance, what performing activity A costs us is the sacrifice of the utility that we could obtain by performing activity B. The two activities involve a cost and have a value, even if they do not imply any painful effort. In its alternative-use formulation cost becomes quite a general phenomenon which is implicit in any genuine act of choice.

Whenever we have to decide how to employ a unit of a resource, we value the benefit that the resource would have in each use, and therefore the value of the resource itself in that particular use. Given these evaluations, we try to allocate the resource in that use where it has the highest (subjective) value and involves the lowest opportunity cost. In other words, we try to allocate the resource in such a way as to equalize the value of the resource in each use. In a market economy, this tendency to equalize the subjective value of the resource in each use will be obtained by the utility-maximizing behaviour of the resource-owners, who will allocate the resource where it is more highly valued. Wieser underlines how value has therefore two services to perform in a market economy. The first is to act 'as title to personal income' (1893, p. 162). The other service of value – and one usually quite overlooked – concerns the 'economical balancing or weighting of goods against goods, and of employment of goods against employment of goods, without regard to distribution among persons, and simply with a view to reach the greatest possible economic results' (p. 162). Wieser stresses that to this service of value belong 'those principles which are absolutely indispensable to any economy' (p. 60), and he accuses the socialists of overlooking this second function of value. In his book *Natural Value*, he intended to correct this fundamental oversight.

'Natural value' was defined by Wieser as 'that value which arises from the social relation between amount of goods and utility or value as it would exist in the communist state' (p. 60). Under communism, not only will goods still have value in so far as they are insufficient for the full satisfaction of the social wants, but also, the institutional conditions of communism will have the advantage of showing the essence of value in its pure form. In a Robinson Crusoe economy, value expresses only the subjective importance that the various goods have for the single individual. By contrast, in a capitalist economy the demands of the goods by members of society, and the evaluation that individuals give to the various goods, depends not only on their needs but also on the distribution of wealth which, by influencing demand, influences also value. The 'Robinson Crusoe analysis' of value therefore can be extended only imperfectly to the capitalist economy, while communism, defined as 'a completely organic and most highly rational community' (p. 61), where the problem of the distribution of wealth does not arise, allows this extension.

Up to a certain point, Wieser's criticism of the socialists as not having understood the double role of value is unjustified. We have already seen that, also according to Marx, value has an allocative function. Marx's criticism of the Ricardian socialists concerned itself mainly with the fact that their system of just exchanges would have simply prevented the market values from coordinating economic decisions (see chapter 3, section 1.1). From this point of view, the 'law of costs' is understood similarly by Marx and Wieser. According to both economists, the discrepancy between costs and market value is useful, as it signals to the economic agents of a market economy where the resources should be employed in order to satisfy the needs of members of society.

Moreover, we have seen how, like Wieser, Marx was well aware of the fact that value was also present in a Robinson Crusoe economy and that it would have had a similarly important allocative function in an early socialist economy (see chapter 3, section 1.4).

However, there is an important difference between Marx and Wieser. While, according to the former, value is linked with the notion that products cost painful labour, according to the latter, cost is not linked with pain. In the opportunity-cost framework, manpower, like other non-human means of production, has a cost in so far as it is available in a limited quantity in relation to our needs, even if its exertion involves no painful effort. Wieser could not, therefore, accept the statement that value exists only under a Marxian model of early socialism, since, even under an advanced communist society, some means of production could still be scarce.

We can see that here Wieser has some good points against Marx (or rather against the classical theory of value).[7] In particular, it is very difficult to think of any possible human society in which time is not scarce. This is true not only because of the fact that human life is limited, but also because it is impossible to do many things at the same time. This means that, even if the other means of production are available in infinite quantities and human activity does not involve any effort, there is still a cost in pursuing any course of action, owing to the fact that other courses of actions cannot be pursued at the same time. In any society, even under the Marxian model of communism, we must choose, and any true choice involves a cost – and therefore a value, according to Wieser's definition.

5   Conclusion

The fact that, in the theory of opportunity cost, cost can occur quite independently of painful labour and is linked to the phenomenon of scarcity does not, of course, imply that in these theories labour can be treated as any other resource.

Wieser and Böhm-Bawerk were, or had become, aware of this fact. Wieser believed that the fact that the exertion of manpower affected human welfare directly (and not just indirectly, as iron or wood affects the welfare of the individuals only via their products) was an important circumstance which distinguished the problem of the allocation and evaluation of manpower from that of the other means of production (1893, pp. 196–9). Furthermore, we have seen that the disagreement between Edgeworth and Marshall on the one hand and Böhm-Bawerk on the other was finally clarified to be a problem related more to the role that the preferences of the workers could have in a capitalist economy than to the existence of these preferences.

However, we will see that, in spite of this consensus about the peculiar nature of human resources, modern economic theory was to be characterized by an almost complete ignorance of the difference between human labour and the other resources. This ignorance is somewhat hard to explain if we do not consider that the approach of modern economic theory has been influenced not so much by the views of the Austrian or English school and their interesting debates dealing with this issue, but by the views of the third stream of the marginalist revolution: that is, by the Lausanne school (or general equilibrium school) of Leon Walras, which we shall examine in the following chapter.

Notes

1   See Collison Black's introduction to Jevons (1970, pp. 14 and 18). Referring to Jevons, Robbins (1970, p. 169) maintains: 'Yet if one is asked precisely to define the exact nature of his achievement, the answer is not easy. He formed no school. He created no system. He died early,

and few of his many brilliant ideas were worked out with the care and precision which, in our treacherous and elusive subject, alone can assume permanent validity.' See also Stigler (1968) and Robbins (1936).

2   I have reported unchanged Jevons's own formulation.

3   Jevons denotes work-time by t and the amount of labour (as meaning the aggregate balance of pain accompanying it') by l; see p. 193 of Jevons (1970).

4   This is pointed out by Louis Schneider in his Introduction to Menger (1963, p. 12). Schneider compares Hayek's reverential attitude to the products of spontaneous social growth with the approach of Menger. In Menger's approach, Schneider observes, these products can embody both the bad and the good aspects of human nature and can therefore be improved by the conscious intervention of society.

5   On the role of methodological individualism in Menger and, in general, in the Austrian approach, see Zamagni (1982). Although the Austrian did not make any use of mathematics, this model can be formalized. An interesting formalization of the Austrian approach is put forward by Karl Menger (the son of Carl Menger: see Menger, 1973).

6   See Marshall (1979, pp. 438, esp. n. 1, where he explicitly criticizes Böhm-Bawerk, and 442, esp. n. 1, where he again criticizes Böhm-Bawerk).

7   We have seen in chapter 2 how the idea that labour is a source of value because it is a source of pain is also shared by both Smith and Ricardo.

6

The perfect socialist society of Leon Walras

1   *Wealth or justice?*

Although Walrasian economics has been so successful that modern mainstream economics is often identified with the developments and the elaboration of the Walrasian system, Walras's *Elements of Pure Economics* was translated into English only in 1954, and his other two books, *Etudes D'Economie Sociale* (1896) and *Etudes D'Economie Politique Appliquée* (1898) are still untranslated and rarely read. Yet is is very hard to disagree with W. Jaffé, who translated Walras's *Elements* into English and has written an invaluable series of work on Walras (see Jaffé, 1967, 1975, 1977, 1978, 1980), that a correct understanding of the *Elements* requires the knowledge of Walras's other books.

The division of Walras's work into three books is related to his intention to divide economics into three distinct subjects, characterized by different but not inconsistent aims. This division relies on a classification of facts based on the distinction between human and natural phenomena and on the distinction between institutional and industrial phenomena. As to the first of these distinctions, Walras observes that it is possible

> to divide the facts of our universe into two categories: those which result from the play of the blind and ineluctable forces of nature and those which result from the exercise of the human will, a force that is free and cognitive. Facts of the first category are found in nature, and that is why we call them natural phenomena. Facts of the second category are found in man, and that is why we call them human phenomena. (Walras, 1977 ed, p. 61)

The distinction between institutional and industrial phenomena further divides human phenomena into two (sub-)categories.

The category of industry includes those (human) phenomena 'which are manifestations of the human will, i.e., human actions in respect to natural forces', whereas the category of institutions includes the (human) phenomena 'that result from the impact of human will or of human actions on the will or actions of other men'. While the first category 'comprises the relations between persons and things', the second 'comprises the relations between persons and persons' (1977, p. 63).

According to Walras, this distinction of human phenomena into two categories gives us the possibility of formulating a precise distinction between *applied economics* and *social economics*. Applied economics is 'the theory of economic production of social wealth, that is, of the organisation of industry under a system of division of labour' (p. 76). Consequently, applied economics is the theory of the organization of industry, and 'industry has a twofold aim: first, to increase the number of useful things which exist only in limited quantities, and second, to transform indirect utilities into direct utilities' (p. 73). 'In pursuing this twofold aim,' Walras observes, 'man performs two distinct classes of operations'. 'The first consists of industrial operations in the narrow sense, that is, *technical* operations', while 'the second class of operations are those related to the *economic* organisation of industry properly speaking' (pp. 73, 74). Unlike the first class, this second class of operations includes the problem of the organization of the division of labour. The two classes of operations are unified, however, by the fact that in both cases the aim of the organization of production is material well-being. 'Moreover.' Walras adds,

> *technical* production and *economic production*, as we have defined them, are not unlike in essence. The two phenomena are, in fact, closely connected and interrelated, each being complementary to the other. Not only are they human and not natural, but they are also both industrial and not social phenomena, for economic production as well as technical production are manifestations of relations between persons and things, with a view to the subordination of the purpose of things to the purposes of persons. (Walras, 1977, p. 76)

In conclusion, applied economics 'defines those relations between man and things which aim at the increase and transformation of social wealth and determine the conditions of an abundant production of social wealth within a community' (p. 79).

Social economics is defined by Walras as the 'science of the distribution of wealth' and deals with the problem of property. While applied economics, or the theory of the production of wealth, is concerned with relations between persons and things, social economics studies the relations between persons and persons. Moreover, while the aim of applied economics is to state the conditions of an abundant production of social wealth, the object of social economics is to establish 'human relations so as to achieve a mutual coordination of human destinies in conformity with reason and justice' (p. 79). Hence, according to Walras, justice is the guiding principle of the science of the distribution of social wealth or social economics. In discussing justice, he makes a distinction between 'commutative justice and distributive justice'. (On this distinction see Walras, 1896, pp. 26 and 209.) Commutative justice requires 'acts of voluntary exchange in which the market value received is equal to the market value given upon thus excluding money gains to any party from trading' (Jaffé, 1980, p. 532). Distributive justice is realized by applying the principle of the *droit naturel*, which implies that the personal resources of each individual should belong to the individual himself and that other natural resources should belong to the state (see Walras, 1896, pp. 214, 218, 266).

The relation between commutative justice and distributive justice is as follows. Commutative justice does not imply the existence of distributive justice, since 'fair exchanges' can occur even when human and natural resources have been distributed initially without following the principle of the *droit naturel*; by contrast, commutative justice is an important requirement in order for an initially just distribution of resources to be perpetuated over time (i.e., not to be upset by unfair relationships of exchange). Only in a system characterized by 'commutative justice' can the principles of distributive justice be successfully applied; only in this case will the working of the system of exchange relations not upset the initial just distribution of resources.

Summing up, social economics and the theory of production of social wealth (or applied economics) study two different sets of human phenomena and are characterized by different aims. The theory of production studies the relations between persons and things and its aim is to determine the relations under which social wealth increases the most. Social economics studies the relations between persons and persons and its aim is to determine the relations of property under which the principles of justice are realized. But are the aims of the theory of production and the aims of social economics compatible? Could the aim of increasing social wealth be incompatible with the relations among persons required by the application of the principles of justice? The existence of such incompatibility could make the results of each one of these disciplines quite useless individually. Further studies (and choices) could be required to decide which of the results achieved following these two aims should be sacrificed. More important, if such incompatibility exists, each human society would always have to face the unfortunate dilemma of choosing between the aim of increasing material wealth and the aim of achieving social justice. The solution of this problem, illustrated at the end of the first four introductory chapters of the *Elements* (1977, p. 79), can be considered the most important aim of Walras's 'pure economics'.

2   *The* socialisme synthetique *answer*

'According to me', Walras writes in his *Etudes D'Economie Politique Appliquée*,

> moral science, which speaks in the name of natural law, has priority over applied economics, which speaks in the name of social interest, and ... moral or economic science is founded in order to formulate the ideal conditions of a society which will be perfect according to all the relations.... (Walras, 1898, p. 274)

This quotation confirms Jaffé's statement (1980, p. 530) that the '*Elements* was intended to be and is, in all but the name, a realistic Utopia' and not 'a model, by the use of which we can examine how the capitalist system works', as Morishima has maintained in his book, *Walras's Economics: A Pure Theory of Capital and Money* (1977, p. 4). The aim of Walras's Utopia is to show that it is possible to conceive of an ideal world which is able to demonstrate that justice and social interest (or material welfare) are two distinct but not inconsistent aims, since in principle they could both be achieved in this Utopian construction.

At first sight it may be surprising, given this self-declared aim of the *Elements*, that Walras conceives of pure economics not as a discipline concerned with human phenomena, similar to social or applied economics, but as a science concerned with natural phenomena, and that he maintains that the pure theory of economics is 'a physico-mathematical science like mechanics or hydrodynamics' (1977, p. 71). However, when we remember the distinction (outlined in the preceding section) that Walras makes between human and natural phenomena, and consider the actual results of Walrasian 'pure economics', any surprise or perplexity may be easily overcome.

Recall that, according to Walras, facts are natural whenever they result from the play of forces of nature and not from the exercise of human will. This does not however imply that we have no control over them. 'Because gravity is a natural phenomenon and obeys natural laws, it does not follow that all we can do is to watch it operate. We can either resist it or give it free rein, whichever we please, but we cannot change its essence or its laws' (Walras, 1977, p. 69). We can see immediately how the first important economic law that appears in the *Elements* can (by Walrasian definition) be considered as a natural law in one respect and as a law occurring in an ideal world non-existent in reality in another respect. Such a law is Walras's independent restatement of Jevons's and Menger's (also independent) propositions that, in a competitive market economy, prices of commodities are proportional to marginal utilities. Walras formulates this law using the term '*rareté*' instead of the term 'marginal utility'. 'Given two commodities in a market,' he maintains, 'each holder attains maximum satisfaction of the last wants satisfied by each of these goods, or the ratio of their *raretés*, is equal to the price' (p. 125).

According to Walras, this law is a natural law. Whenever certain conditions, such as the existence of competitive markets, are satisfied, the maximizing behaviour of the commodity holders will imply that the ratio of the *rareté* of two commodities equals their *rareté* or marginal utilities. As with the law of gravity, this law can be either resisted or given free rein, but its essence cannot be changed. 'It would be even possible, in an extreme case', Walras observes, 'to abolish value altogether by abolishing exchange' (p. 69). Yet when exchange is allowed and competitive markets are formed, prices of commodities will tend to be proportional to their *raretés*. As with other natural laws, the law of value works under certain ideal conditions, and its natural character or its independence from human will lies in the fact that it necessarily holds true whenever those conditions are satisfied, and not in the fact that we cannot change them.

On the other hand, Walras believed that the *Elements* was intended to formulate the ideal conditions for a Utopian society, one that is perfect according to all relations and, at least in principle, would be greatly different from any existing society. Immediately we can see how this Utopian character of the *Elements* is perfectly compatible with the natural character of the law of value. Perfectly competitive markets may exist nowhere, and may be only the description of conditions for a Utopian society; but this does not prevent us from describing the 'natural laws' that would characterize that society.

At this point we will consider how Walras extends the proposition examined above to a market in which productive services (in particular, labour) are exchanged and used for producing consumption goods, and how a world characterized by competitive markets can conciliate the aims of maximizing material welfare and justice, or the aims of applied and social economics.

Menger and Jevons held two different points of view about the influence that work performed has on the welfare of an individual (chapter 5, sections 1 and 2). According to Menger, work affects welfare only indirectly, through the production of consumption goods, whereas for Jevons the type and the amount of work performed affect the welfare of an individual directly. The way in which Walras assumes that work affects welfare deserves greater attention, since his treatment of this problem has acted as a successful compromise between the Austrian and English approach (see section 4 below). In addition, the assumption has been inherited by modern economics and has conditioned its results in a negative way, according to the writer (see section 4 below and chapter 7).

Walras observes that the productive services of resources (including the productive service of personal resources, i.e., labour) can be either consumed by the individuals that own them, or sold to other individuals. Let us consider the case of a productive service t (the productive service of the 'human capital' of an individual). Each individual who has initial endowment q_t of t can offer a quantity 0_t of this service. 0_t is positive when it represents a quantity offered and negative when it represents a quantity demanded. The amount of the productive service q_t that an individual consumes is therefore equal to

$$q_t - 0_t.$$

Walras assumes that its *rareté* or marginal utility functions (and therefore utility) are affected not only by the consumption of products, but also by the quantity $(q_t - O_t)$ consumed by each individual (see Walras, 1977, lesson 20, esp. p. 238). In the case of labour, the welfare of an individual is assumed to be affected by that part of himself that he consumes. By contrast, it is not assumed that the welfare of an individual is affected by that part of labour that he has offered and sold on the market. In the last section of this chapter we will consider the way in which this formulation differs from those of Jevons and Mengers, and also its shortcomings. For the time being, it is sufficient to point out that the consumption of productive services affects the welfare of each individual exactly in the same way as any other consumption good affects it. This characteristic of the Walrasian approach implies that the proposition, 'given two commodities in a market, each holder attains maximum satisfaction of wants when the ratio of their *raretés* is equal to price', can include the cases in which the commodities are two products, or two productive services, or a productive service and a product. The preceding statements imply that for each set of prices we can derive the quantity of each product demanded and each productive service offered (i.e., O_t) by each individual, given his *rareté* function and his resource endowments. For each set of prices, therefore, we can determine the total demands of products and the total supplies of productive services simply by summing.

Walras completes his system of equations by assuming the existence of an equilibrium situation, where 'the quantities of productive services used are equal to the quantities effectively used' and where 'the selling prices of products are equal to the cost of the productive services' (1977, p. 240). This system enables us to determine the prices and the quantities exchanged and produced of the various commodities, given tastes (i.e., the *rareté* functions), technology and the *initial resource endowments of the individuals*. In this economic equilibrium, price ratios equal *rareté* ratios and therefore individuals achieve the maximum satisfaction of wants. This induces Walras to give a first intuitive statement regarding the well-known optimality properties of a competitive equilibrium:

> Production in a market ruled by free competition is an operation by which services can be combined and converted into products of such nature and in such quantities as will give the greatest possible satisfaction of wants within the

> limits of the double condition, that each service and each product have only one price in the market, namely the price at which the quantity supplied equals the quantity demanded, and that the selling price of the products be equal to the cost of services employed in making them. (Walras, 1977, p. 255)

This proposition is probably the most important one in the *Elements of Pure Economics* if not in the whole Walrasian system. As we will see, it is intended to show that the aim of maximizing material welfare and the aim of justice are not inconsistent, and that pure economics, applied economics and social economics can constitute three separate fields assessing notions that are not incompatible. The relationship between applied economics and this proposition is immediately put forward in the *Elements*. Walras observes that, from the point of view of pure science, competition has been treated as a datum, and 'it did not matter whether or not we observed it in the real world' (p. 255).

> It was in this light that we studied the nature, causes and consequences of free competition. We now know that these consequences may be summed up as the attainment, within certain limits, of maximum utility. Hence, free competition becomes a principle or a rule of practical significance, so that it only remains to extend the application of this rule to agriculture, industry and trade. Thus the conclusions of pure science bring us to the very threshold of applied science. (Walras, 1977, p. 255)

Walras is well aware of the limitations that exist for the applicability of this theorem and he observes that competition cannot work in the cases of natural monopolies and public goods. The task of applied economics is to distinguish between the cases in which competition is applicable and those in which it is not, the latter of which will require state intervention in production. In the cases in which competition is applicable, the task of applied economics is to abolish all the obstacles that could prevent competition from doing its job. The result of competition is the attainment of maximum utility – which is exactly the aim of applied economics. Is this aim consistent with the aim of social economics, i.e., justice?

We have seen that competition gives the greatest possible satisfaction within the limitations of two conditions: first, all exchanges must be performed at market equilibrium prices;

and second, the selling prices of the products must equal their production costs. These conditions imply that we must be in an equilibrium situation where no profits or losses can be realized by the entrepreneurs as a result of an excess demand or excess supply of certain products. These same two conditions are required by commutative justice. Walras explicitly mentions them in his *Etudes d'Economie Sociale*, where he observes that 'the condition that there is only one price running on the market is well a condition of justice', and 'the condition that the produces are manufactured at the lowest possible price is also a condition of justice' (1896, p. 212). It follows that the attainment of maximum utility and commutative justice are perfectly consistent, since they require the existence of the very same conditions on the market. As to distributive justice, Walras points out that the proposition that free competition can achieve a maximum of utility is true only as regards a certain set of property rights. Within this same proposition, the question of distributive justice is completely left to one side 'since our sole object has been to show how a certain (initial) distribution of services gives rise to a certain distribution of products' (p. 257). (See also Walras, 1896, p. 209). He explicitly criticizes those 'economists, who, not content with exaggerating the applicability of laissez-faire, laissez-passer to industry, even extend it to the completely extraneous question of property' (1977, p. 257). On the other hand, exchanges at market equilibrium prices are compatible with commutative justice. This implies that, if the initial distribution of productive services follows the principles of the *droit naturel*, the consequent distribution of products will also be consistent with the principles of distributive justice. The attainment of maximum utility is clearly different from the achievement of distributive justice but it is not incompatible with it. By contrast, since the attainment of maximum utility requires market exchanges at equilibrium prices, thus implying the existence of commutative justice, it also implies a situation where an initial just distribution can be perpetuated over time.

We have seen that the Walrasian *droit naturel* implies that, while personal resources should belong to the individual, natural resources should belong to the state. We have also seen that, according to Walras, competitive markets and individual initiative can efficiently provide private goods but will fail to provide public goods. These two considerations cause Walras to propose that the state could rent the natural resources to the individuals and finance the production of public goods by the incomes obtained from these rents (1896, p. 236). In his 'Théorie de la Propriété' (p. 205), Walras calls the theory that he proposes 'socialisme synthetique. (p. 239). By socialisme synthetique he means a society that operates a synthesis between the rights of the individual and the rights of the state, in both the economic and the social fields.

Walras compares the society that he proposes to the collectivist society proposed by Marx and his followers (see chapter 3 above, esp. sections 1.3 and 1.4). He describes how the first source for a disagreement between his own approach and the collectivist approach lies in the theory of value held by the Marxists, according to which labour is the only source of value. Like the Austrian approach, which we examined in the preceding chapter, the Walrasian approach relates the value of resources to their scarcity. Therefore both labour and natural resources have value in so far as they are scarce. By contrast, Walras believes that he can find a common ground with the collectivist approach within his double statement that personal resources should belong to the individual and natural resources to the state.

Yet, another cause for disagreement with the collectivist approach can be the question of the property of produced capital goods. Walras believes that, in the future, society-produced capital goods (capitaux artificiels), as well as personal and natural resources, should have a value related to their scarcity (and for the same reasons). Moreover, he believes that these capital goods should belong to the state only when they have been produced by using the rents earned by the state (which owns natural resources), but should belong to individuals when they have been financed by the wages of workers. He observes that the collectivists would object to allowing the private property of a part of the produced capital to exist; by so doing, we would run the risk of recreating (in the future society) the financial aristocracy that oppresses us in the present society. However, Walras believes that this danger will not exist in the future socialist society that he proposes. There, the causes of and conditions for the development of this financial aristocracy are suppressed because real estate property and monopolies are not allowed. By contrast, in our present society real estate property allows its owners to become increasingly rich since the rareté of real estate is constantly increasing in a developing society. Moreover, artificial and natural monopolies allow their holders 'to fix the quantity produced in such a way to have a differential, and the maximum differential, between selling price and cost' (1896, p. 237). Walras states that all the big fortunes have been accumulated under these two conditions: their abolition should prevent their creation in his model of a socialist society, wherein persons' capitals can derive only from their individual savings; that is, from an excess of wages over consumption. Under socialism these private capitals will have the aim of preparing a more sure future and a serene retirement for the workers while increasing the availability of resources currently employed (see Walras, 1896, p. 238).

In conclusion, in the Walrasian socialist society, the great part of produced capital belongs to the state while a small part of it belongs to the workers under the form of equities and bonds of enterprises, which are often managed by the workers themselves, and this socialist society achieves the aim both of maximizing the welfare of its members and of realizing just relations among people.

3   Just prices and the ticket economy

The Walrasian model of a 'perfect' socialist society is probably the most complete and consistent Utopian project ever conceived in the history of social sciences. However, there are two important shortcomings of the model which have been a source of confusion among economists. The first is related to the way in which Walras treats the preferences of members of society for their own work. The second concerns a peculiar aspect of this perfect society: that all exchanges and production decisions are assumed to be implemented at market equilibrium prices. We will treat this last problem in this section, while a critique of the way in which Walras describes the preferences for work will be made in section 4.

We have seen that both justice and the maximization of utility require the double condition (1) that each service and each product have only one price in the market (the price at which the quantity supplied equals the quantity demanded), and (2) that the selling price of the products is equal to the cost of services employed in making them. These two conditions can be satisfied only if all exchanges and all the production processes are carried out in a market equilibrium situation (where Walras assumes that the profits of the entrepreneurs disappear). By contrast, we can easily see that this double condition cannot be satisfied if the market is not in equilibrium. In this case, prices will be changing according to the signs of excess demands, and exchanges made at different times will be for different prices. Moreover, even at the same moment of time, different prices can exist in the market since the change in prices is likely to occur in some deals earlier than in others. Therefore the condition that each service and each product must have only one price in the market cannot be satisfied by the working of a real market economy. Such an economy requires price changes (thus, trade at non-equilibrium prices) in order to eliminate the excesses of demand and supply as well as to move in the direction of an equilibrium state.

As to the equality between selling prices of the products and their production costs, a disequilibrium situation implies that some profits are realized when there is excess demand for a certain product and that some losses are suffered by the entrepreneurs who produce any oversupplied product. Therefore, the existence of a disequilibrium situation implies that the selling prices of the products and the costs of services employed in making them are not equal. We have already seen in chapter 3 that these gains and these losses are required by the market mechanism in order for society to move in the direction of an equilibrium state. Only the gains (losses) realized in the production of the goods for which there is an excess demand (supply) can induce the profit-seeking entrepreneurs to produce those goods that are undersupplied and give up the production of the oversupplied commodities.

Thus, the very working of the market mechanism requires that exchanges must be carried out at various prices, prices different in general from that price at which demand equals supply, and that the selling price of products in general must be different from the cost of services employed in making them. Therefore, the two conditions required for the attainment of maximum utility and justice are in general being violated by the working of the real market.

Moreover, even if the market mechanism is able to achieve an equilibrium state, this equilibrium is different from the equilibrium required by Walras, which is obtained under the assumption that no trade and no production occurs at non-market equilibrium prices. Recall that this equilibrium is calculated on the basis of a certain given initial distribution of resource endowments among individuals and therefore a certain initial distribution and total amount of social wealth (see section 2 above). But trading at non-equilibrium prices is very likely to change both this initial distribution and total amount of social wealth, well before exchange and production at equilibrium prices can take place.

The fact that trading at non-equilibrium prices can change the initial distribution of social wealth can be easily understood by observing that individuals who happen to buy certain commodities when their prices are low will see a substantial increase in their wealth when the prices of these commodities increase; while individuals who buy commodities when their price is high will suffer a substantial decrease in their wealth when the price of the commodities falls.

Also, the total wealth of society is unlikely to remain the same when exchange and production can take place at non-equilibrium prices. Production decisions implemented at non-equilibrium prices can easily imply that some products are oversupplied, and, since production is usually an irreversible process, the resources used up in their production cannot be reallocated if the consequent change in prices indicates that there is no demand for these products. Thus, if production can take place at non-equilibrium prices, these resources will have been misallocated and may even have been completely wasted for ever. The working of a market economy can therefore easily imply that the initial endowment of social resources decreases and the total amount of social wealth available to the economy changes.

The fact that the working economy is not characterized by the double condition that all exchanges and production decisions are implemented at equilibrium seems therefore to imply that a market economy cannot satisfy the requirements of the Walrasian perfect society. It seems to fall short of the aims of commutative justice and utility maximization (given certain property rights) because the distribution and the total amount of wealth are changed by the working of the market mechanism. Walras certainly perceived at least some aspects of this problem, but the imaginative solution that he gave to it is certainly not free from ambiguities. In the *Elements* (1977, p. 242) he assumes that equilibrium is achieved by its 'perfect society' in the following way. He imagines that at non-equilibrium prices the agents of the economy use tickets and write down on paper only the amounts of commodities that they are willing to exchange and to produce at those prices. The price of each commodity is then increased (decreased) whenever there is an excess demand (supply) for that commodity. This procedure is repeated several times up to the point at which equilibrium prices are achieved and all the excess demands and supplies have disappeared. Only at these equilibrium prices are the agents of the economy allowed to implement their exchange and production decisions; the latter are then consistent with the aims of attaining maximum utility and justice for the very reason that they have been carried out only in equilibrium.

Walras was certainly aware of the difference between his 'ticket economy' and real market economies; but he thought that his 'ticket economy' could be regarded as an approximation of real-life market economies. Moreover, he believed that market economies could be reformed in such a way as to become closer to his ticket economy in which no exchange and no production was allowed before the achievement of the equilibrium. He thought that an example of such markets could be found in those 'best organized' markets such as the stock exchange, 'where purchases and sales are made by auction, through the instrumentality of stockbrokers, commercial brokers or criers acting as agents who centralise transactions in such a way that the terms of every exchange are openly announced and an opportunity is given to sellers to lower their prices and to buyers to raise their bids' (1977, p. 84). And in his *Etudes D'Economie Politique Appliquée*, Walras observers that markets like the stock exchange 'are organized a little better than the labour market, which is not organized at all' (1898, p. 279), and he wishes for a better organization of all markets, in order that the current prices of the products and productive services could be closer to their equilibrium values.

However, the changes that Walras introduced in the fourth edition of the *Elements* when treating the adjustment process of the stock exchange indicate that he felt that even these 'centralized' markets were rather far from the characteristics required by 'its perfect society'. In that edition, when considering a disequilibrium situation on the stock exchange, where at the current price there is an excess demand, he adds that, 'Theoretically, trading should come to a halt' at that point (p. 85). This indicates the gap existing between the suggestions of the 'pure theory' of the *Elements*, with its normative implications, and the actual working of these 'centralized' markets. And, indeed, the 'centralization' of transactions required by the 'pure theory' implied that an auctioneer had not only the role of making clear to everybody the current price but also the authority of suspending transactions until the equilibrium was achieved. Up to that point, contracts should have been written on paper but not implemented.

The relation between the market economy and the 'ticket economy' is therefore treated in the *Elements* in a rather ambiguous way. On the one hand, the properties of the 'ticket economy' are treated as a close approximation to the properties of the markets, and on the other hand the difference between the two economies is often perceived. In order to understand better this latter difference, it may be useful to go back to the Marxian distinction between market-type and non-market-type coordination and to Marx's criticism of the Ricardian socialists and Proudhon (chapter 2, section 1). This is not a mere coincidence, since Walras shares with Bray, Gray and Proudhon (the work of whom is explicitly quoted in the *Elements*) a common aim and, up to a certain point, a common way of achieving it. We have already seen that the Ricardian socialists intended to realize a society having the same double aim as that of the Walrasian socialist society, i.e., to maximize social wealth and eliminate injustice. Like Walras, they believed that a reformed market system characterized by 'just exchanges' could achieve these goals. Here, however, the ways of Walras and the Ricardian socialists depart. According to the latter, just exchanges are those exchanges of commodities carried out to labour-embodied values, whereas Walras maintains that the 'just price is that which corresponds at a given moment to the equality of the effective supply and demand . . . . (1898, p. 293.)

The fact that the Walrasian just price is defined directly as an equilibrium price avoids one of the shortcomings of the Ricardian socialist definition: that the just price could be incompatible with the existence of an equilibrium (see chapter 3, section 1.1). On the other hand, the Walrasian definition directly acknowledges that just prices in a market economy can occur only in equilibrium – implicitly confirming Marx's criticism that no market economy could in general generate any system of equal or just exchanges. We have also seen that Marx believed that the 'equal exchanges', which the market system failed to achieve because of the *a posteriori* nature of market coordination, could be achieved under a planned system (see chapter 3, sections 1.2 and 1.3). While, under a market, economic decisions were first implemented and then coordinated *a posteriori*, the opposite was true for a planned system, where economic decisions were first coordinated *a priori* and only afterwards implemented. And this *a priori* coordination was necessary in order to have just exchanges and no waste of social resources – an impossible result under the market system (see chapter 3, sections 1.3 and 1.4). Now, if we interpret the Walrasian ticket economy (where an auctioneer cries new prices according to the excess of demand written on paper and allows production and exchange only at equilibrium prices) as an approximate description of a market system, Marx's line of reasoning seems to be seriously challenged by Walras. In this case, Walras would be showing that a market system could achieve results that Marx believed, in general, to be possible only for a planned system.

But it is easy to see that it is impossible to interpret the ticket economy as an approximation of a market system when comparing it with a planned system. The ticket economy is in fact a *planned* and not a market system. In the ticket economy the decisions are first coordinated by an auctioneer and only afterwards, when their consistency has been achieved, implemented. Only at equilibrium are the agents allowed to trade and produce. Before the achievement of equilibrium, agents are allowed to collaborate with the auctioneer only by sending him messages written on paper. In other words, the ticket economy is characterized by the existence of *a priori* coordination and is therefore the description of a possible planned system. The differences that exist between the 'ticket economy' and a market system are therefore very much the same differences that exist between a planned economy, characterized by *a priori* coordination, and the market economy, characterized by *a posteriori* information. And these differences between the ticket and the market economy confirm the insights that Marx had about the differences between a planned and a market economy. While a 'ticket economy' (i.e., a planned economy) can have exchanges and production decisions implemented only at equilibrium price, a market economy cannot avoid having them implemented at non-equilibrium prices.

The ambiguity of Walras, therefore, lies in his presentation of a ticket economy, with its transactions and production decisions centralized by some authority (for instance, an auctioneer), as a first approximation of the working of a market system when the ticket economy is actually a planned system. So Walras can be criticized on the same grounds for which Marx criticized the Ricardian socialists. Like the Ricardian socialists and Proudhon, he did not understand that a planned system, and not a reformed market, was necessary for achieving the double aim of maximizing social welfare and realizing just exchanges.

On the other hand, Walras perceived this problem. His idea that a market system can achieve these aims only by centralizing transactions in the hands of some authority is needed one of insight. It suggests that, on the one hand, an extreme centralization of market transactions brings us to the border of a (decentralized) planned system, and that, on the other hand, an extreme decentranization of a planning system brings us to the border of a (centralized) market system. This suggestion can be very useful if it does not imply that we then forget the institutional differences between market and non-market type coordination, as Walras himself did and as did many other economists (see chapter 8 below, section 1).

4   Work as forgone leisure

We now come to the second ambiguity of the Walrasian system. We have seen that, while Jevons assumed that the utility of the individuals was affected by both the goods consumed and the labour performed by these individuals, Menger assumed that utility was affected only by the goods that these individuals consumed. We have also seen that Walras uses a formulation that is different from both Jevons's and Menger's, assuming that the utility of individuals is influenced by only that part of labour that they consume – 'that part of labour' being either their own labour or the labour of other individuals (see section 2 above). Labour can therefore be treated in the Walrasian formulation as any other consumption good since it affects the utility of the individuals in exactly the same way. Thus, in the Walrasian formulation the labour that an individual performs can be divided into two parts: a part auto-consumed by the individual himself, and a part that is sold and used in the production of consumption goods or consumption services that are consumed by other individuals. The first part, which, following Walras's own suggestion (1977, p. 27 and translator's n. 6) and the tradition of the subsequent literature, we will call 'leisure', is assumed to affect the welfare of the individual. By contrast, the second part, for which we will keep the name of 'labour', is assumed *not* to affect the welfare of the individual.

The Walrasian formulation seems to offer a double advantage. On the one hand, labour can be treated like any other consumption good since it affects utility only in so far as it is consumed as leisure by an individual. This simplifies the analysis quite remarkably, since preferences for labour can be treated by simply increasing the number of consumption goods that affect the utility function. On the other hand, such formulation seems to take into account the fact that the welfare of individuals is also affected by the labour expended in the production of consumption goods. Since each individual is endowed with only a given amount of manpower (for instance, 24 hours), each increase of labour-time expended in production brings about a decrease of leisure-time and therefore a decrease of welfare – the latter circumstance implying that the disutility of labour is taken into account by the Walrasian formulation.

This double advantage of the Walrasian formulation seems to offer an appealing compromise between the approach of Menger and that of Jevons. On the one hand, the Walrasian formulation seems to imply that the Mengerian approach can be held unchanged when the preferences of the individuals for their own labour are taken into account, since this requires only that we consider that the welfare of individuals is affected by one additional consumption good, called 'leisure'. On the other hand, the Walrasian formulation seems to take into account Jevons's idea that the welfare of the individuals is also affected by the painful amount of work which they perform, owing to the fact that we have seen how, in the Walrasian framework, any increase of working-time implies a decrease of the available leisure-time and therefore a reduction of welfare and an increase of disutility.

These advantages, which seem to be offered by the Walrasian formulation, can probably explain how this formulation has become the standard one in modern textbooks. In fact, economists of the generation immediately following that of Edgeworth, Marshall, Böhm-Bawerk and Wieser already regarded their disputes (examined in the preceding chapter, esp. section 3) as rather meaningless. An assumption that leisure and not work affected utility seemed to be a successful compromise between the approaches of Jevons and Menger. For instance, according to Robbins, this discussion (defined by him as a 'battle of giants', more for the importance of the economists involved in it than for its content) had simply paved the way 'for the now almost universal recognition that even when disutilities are taken into account they are ultimately to be regarded as being the pull of forgone leisure or forgone present income – opportunity costs rather than disutilities in the sense of the old hedomistic calculus' (Robbins, 1930, p. 208). A similar opinion was expressed by Schumpeter in his *History of Economic Analysis* (1953), where he argued that not one of the participants gained too much from the dispute, and that, 'Moreover, if we attach enough importance to having our value theory based upon utility only, all we have to do is to replace disutility of labour by the utility of leisure' (p. 924). In a footnote, he added that this was to be recommended in any case since this device made the analysis easier (p. 924, n. 9).[1]

In spite of the almost universal success obtained among more recent generations of economists, the Walrasian formulation is, in my opinion, a very misleading device. We can easily show that using this 'leisure device' is tantamount to assuming that the workers care only for the amount of their labour used up in production and not for the way in which a given amount of their labour is allocated among different productive uses (i.e., different tasks). We have already seen that the use of this 'leisure device' does not imply that workers are assumed to be indifferent towards the amount of work that they perform, and that it is for this reason that such a device is usually defended. But we can easily see that using this 'leisure device' implies that we implicitly assume that the workers are indifferent to the kind of activity that they perform in production. Let us in fact assume that a *given* amount of a worker's labour is allocated in a given way in production among certain given alternative productive uses. As a consequence, the worker consumes a certain given amount of leisure-time. For example, let us assume that our worker works in the celebrated pin-making factory (see chapter 1) for a given amount of time – say, 8 hours – and that this amount of manpower is allocated in two different productive uses – say, drawing the wire and cutting it – and that she has to perform each one of these activities for 4 hours. In this example, the leisure-time that is available to the worker is equal to 16 hours (i.e., 24 hours–8 hours), and obviously any change in the length of the working day implies a change of the available leisure time and therefore a change of the level of welfare of the worker. On the other hand, any change in the allocation of the manpower of the worker expended in production is assumed to leave the welfare of the worker unchanged. If, for instance, in our example the allocation of the worker in production is changed and the worker has to draw the wire for 2 hours and cut it for 6 hours instead of performing each task for 4 hours, her welfare is implicitly assumed to be unchanged since the available leisure-time is still the same (i.e., 16 hours). Thus, the use of the leisure device that is implicit in the Walrasian formulation is tantamount to assuming that the workers are indifferent among alternative allocations of their manpower in production – that is, indifferent to the kind of work that they perform.

Walras treats human labour in a way very similar to that of Ricardo, Mill and the Ricardian socialists. Like Ricardo, he acknowledges only one source of non-homogeneity of labour (that arising from differences of skill), while he ignores its other important source: the fact that the different uses of labour can give quite different levels of (dis)utility to the worker for the very fact that, when a worker is selling her manpower, she is also selling a piece of her life and cannot be indifferent to the way in which this piece of life is going to be spent.

Using the Marxian terminology, Walras is implicitly assuming, in using his leisure device, that labour is abstract (i.e., homogeneous).[2] We have already seen in chapter 3 how Marx also uses this assumption and justifies it. The difference between Marx, who explicitly discusses the limits and the institutional frameworks under which this assumption holds, and Walras, who implicitly adopts it, is however striking.

Marx says that the fact that under capitalism production is organized according to certain rules, based on the employment contract and the profit-maximizing behaviour of the capitalists, implies that a very detailed division of labour is introduced under this institutional framework, which in turn implies that the large majority of productive tasks become equally routine and similar among themselves. This similarity can well imply that under capitalism (and also under an early stage of socialism) the workers are almost indifferent to these productive tasks, which have all been made equally painful and uninteresting by the profit-maximizing behaviour of the capitalists (see chapter 3, esp. diagram (F1)). Under capitalism, the assumption of homogeneous or abstract labour can therefore be a good approximation to reality. On the other hand, Marx, like Smith and Jevons, is well aware that individuals have preferences for the kinds of activity they perform in production. Marx's final Utopian project takes these preferences into account, since the main characteristic of a communist society is to transform what was abstract labour under capitalism into an enjoyable activity (chapter 3, section 2.3).

By contrast, in the Walrasian approach the assumption of abstract labour becomes an implicit characteristic of a Utopian perfect society, on the basis of which some normative rules can be deduced. Labour becomes homogeneous not because of any particular characteristic of the labour process, but simply because it is implicitly assumed that individuals are indifferent about the allocation of their manpower in production. The normative rules that can follow via this approach are therefore in deep contrast to the rules that can follow the Marxian approach. While Marx considers the indifference of subjects towards their work an historical circumstance that has to be changed, Walras implicitly considers this indifference as an assumption from which some normative rules can be deduced for building a perfect society.

In conclusion, the Walrasian approach is seriously handicapped by the restrictive assumption that the members of society consider the consumption of goods and leisure time their only ends while they regard their own work only as a means for achieving these ends and are otherwise indifferent to its allocation. Kant (1949, p. 178) considered the rule, 'Act so as to treat man, in your own person as well as in that of anyone else, always as an end, never merely as means', as one of the founding rules of ethics.

Modern economics, by accepting the Walrasian approach, has also accepted an implicit rule, which implies that members of society can be treated as producers in the opposite way: always as a means only, and never as an end in themselves. This implicit rule, by ignoring the preferences and needs of people as producers, can only be the foundation of other rules which dictate the allocation of people in production, quite independently of their wills. This set of rules, which I will call the 'rules of the dictatorship of economics', are the object of the next chapter and can be a serious obstacle to an extension of democracy to economic life.

Notes

1   By contrast, a Smithian standpoint is taken by Blaug (1972), who insightfully argues that 'The workers' decision to enter an occupation is not a marginal choice and for that reason there seems to be a fundamental non-parallelism between the allocation of human and non-human resource.' The 'choice between different occupations is in fact an either-or decision' (p. 494).

2   See chapter 3, sections 2.2 and 2.3, where the Marxian concept of homogeneous or abstract labour is explained.

7

The rules of economic dictatorship

Modern orthodox economic theory has inherited from Walras the (often implicit) assumption that the welfare of the individuals is affected directly only by the time they consume as leisure and not by work-time. As in Walras, this assumption has been used to state how a society *should* organize production and to deduce some rules that society should follow in order to maximize social welfare.

In orthodox economic theory, the conceptual framework underlying the resource allocation model characterizes society as one large organization. The allocation model is then used to study the conditions under which this organization is able to attain maximum welfare. The allocation model is typically structured as a constrained maximization problem. The objective function is implicitly formulated to represent the preferences for alternative states of the economy. Its arguments are constrainted by exogenously given resources and production technology. For example, a general formulation of the standard maximization problem would be:

$$\text{maximize } U(\mathbf{y})$$

$$\text{subject to } F(\mathbf{y}; \mathbf{x}) = 0.$$

The function $U(\mathbf{y})$ is a social welfare function defined over output of goods y_i where $y \in R_+^n$; and where the production possibility frontier, denoted by the function $F(\mathbf{y}, \mathbf{x}) = 0$, describes an implicit relation between the vector of outputs $\mathbf{y}$ and the vector of total given inputs $\mathbf{x}$.

A characteristic common to variations of this general model is that a distinction is made between inputs and outputs; and it is the latter that are desired, i.e., the vector y is the argument of the social welfare function. If a resource that is employed as an input in production is at the same time positively (or negatively) desired, it is usual to introduce a reservation activity by which an amount of the resource can be converted into an equal amount of a desired good. Koopmans (1951) refers to this as a semantic device: 'By this semantic device, we transfer the desirability properties that a primary factor might originally possess to a final commodity introduced for that purpose.'[1] The resource can then be used either in production or as an input in the reservation activity. Thus, by means of the semantic device, we have preserved the distinction between outputs, desired goods, and inputs, non-desired goods.

We can easily see how, by this semantic device, 'leisure' can therefore be considered a final commodity introduced for the purpose of transferring onto it the desirability properties that labour might originally possess. We have already seen (in section 4 of the preceding chapter) that this 'leisure semantic device' that modern economics (similar to Walras) accepts is tantamount to assuming that members of society are indifferent as to the allocation of their manpower among alternative tasks. In the following section this criticism is restated in the framework of a specification of the general resource allocation model outlined above; and a reformulation of the traditional social welfare function, which takes into account the fact that workers do have preferences about the allocation of their own manpower, is constrasted to the traditional one.

In section 3 this criticism is then applied to the old matter of the division of labour. If the 'leisure device' is adopted, de-skilling jobs (i.e. organizing the production process in such a way that each job contains fewer tasks) improves social welfare. Since profit-maximizing (or even output-maximizing) behaviour requires that a given amount of manpower must be allocated by de-skilling jobs, profit-maximizing managers act consistently with social welfare maximization. When workers' preferences are taken into account, however, de-skilling no longer necessarily improves social welfare.

Section 4 criticizes the conventional notion of technological efficiency on the grounds that the latter is a necessary condition for maximizing social welfare only when the 'leisure device' is adopted. A common conclusion of these two sections is that in general two simple rules – (1) de-skill jobs whenever this is possible; (2) improve technological efficiency – which are implied by profit-maximizing behaviour,[2] are not necessarily consistent with social welfare maximization.

Section 5 examines the issues of decentralization. When the restrictive 'leisure device' is not adopted, the internal allocation of manpower within the firms cannot be left to the 'profit-maximizing managers' and should be handled entirely through market transactions at equilibrium prices. The internal allocation of the profit-maximizing managers is in fact inconsistent with social welfare maximization. Also, a third rule – (3) allocate labour within the firm by profit-maximizing – is not therefore in general consistent with the maximization of social welfare when the preferences of the workers for their own work are taken into account.

In the concluding section, it is maintained that each of these three rules contains some elements that can favour an economic dictatorship based on rules suggested by an 'economic science' which ignores the needs of the individuals as producers.

2 *The leisure device and workers' preferences*

We will start by giving three definitions which will be used in the following pages. These are the concepts of task, job and skill.

Definition 2.1 A task is a use in production of manpower. It defines not only the work to be done, but also how it is to be done, and the time allowed to do it. By keeping fixed the 'what' and 'how' components of a task, we measure the task in units (time) of manpower. We will denote by x_{ij} the amount of task j to be performed in firm i; there are T possible tasks. Thus a T-tuple $x_i \in R^T$ defines the set of the tasks to be performed in the production process of firm i; typically, $x_{ij} = 0$ for some $j \in [1, \dots, T]$.

Definition 2.2 A job J_α^i in firm i is a subset of the set of tasks x_i to be performed by one unit of manpower. The set of jobs $[J_\alpha^i]$ in firm i defines the firm's organization of production.

For example, suppose that in firm i there are four tasks to be performed, x_{i1}, x_{i2}, x_{i3} and x_{i4}; then examples of possible types of organization of production are:

(i)   there exists one job, J_1^i, defined by $[x_{i1}, x_{i2}, x_{i3}, x_{i4}]$;
(ii) there exists two jobs, J_1^i, J_2^i; J_1^i, defined by $[x_{i1}, x_{i2}]$ and j_2^i defined by $[x_{i3}, x_{i4}]$;

(iii)   there exists four jobs, J_1^i, J_2^i, J_3^i, J_4^i, each defined by one task, x_{ij}, respectively.

Definition 2.3   A skill is the resource endowment of a worker, and is defined by the set of tasks that one unit of manpower is able to perform. If we denote by X the set of all possible tasks to be performed in the economy, i.e. $x_{ij} \in X$ for all i, j, then a skill S_k would be a subset of X.

Suppose that, as in the above example, $X = x_{i1},\ x_{i2},\ x_{i3},\ x_{i4}$; then possible types of skill would be:

(i) S_1 defined by the ability to perform at least $x_{i1}, x_{i2}, x_{i3}, x_{i4}$;
(ii) S_2 defined by the ability to perform at least x_{i1}, x_{i2}, x_{i3};
(iii) S_3 defined by the ability to perform at least x_{i1}, x_{i2};
(iv) S_4 defined by the ability to perform at least x_{i3}, x_{i4}.

As to the production side of the economy, we will make assumptions that are very similar to the ones that are traditionally made in resource allocation models. As in those models, we will assume that each product is produced by only one 'representative' firm. This simplifying assumption does not do any analytical damage if we keep in mind that firm i stands for 'many firms' of type i. Firms of a different type are assumed to produce (at least slightly) different products, and each firm is assumed to produce only one product. Moreover, on the one hand we will make the analysis simpler by assuming that manpower is the only input that is used in production; on the other hand we will explicitly consider the situation in which several tasks are used in each production process and several different kinds of manpower (skills) exist in the economy. The following assumptions are therefore made.

Assumption 2.1   A production process exists for the production of each produced good $y_1, \ldots, y_n$. Let $f_i(x_i)$ denote the production process for good i, where x_i is a vector of tasks, measured in manpower units. We shall further assume that there are no production indivisibilities and no joint production, and that the marginal productivity of a task j in firm i is non-negative; i.e.,

$$\frac{\partial f_i(x_i)}{\partial x_{ij}} \geqslant 0 \quad i = 1, \ldots, n \quad j = 1, \ldots, T.$$

Assumption 2.2   Assume that there exist v skills in the economy $[S_1, \ldots, S_v]$ with resource endowment measured in units of manpower; i.e., $[L_1, \ldots, L_v]$.

Furthermore, we will follow Arrow and Hahn's (1971) generalization of Koopman's semantic device by making the following assumption.

Assumption 2.3   For each skill k in the economy, there exists a reservation activity by which any amount of manpower units with skill k, x_{0k} can be converted into an equal amount of leisure time y_{0k}; i.e., $y_{0k} = x_{0k}$; x_{0k} will be considered to be a task that skill k is able to perform; hence X will now contain x_{0k} for all k and the set of tasks defining S_k will include x_{0k}.

As for the preferences of society, we will assume that they can be completely ordered by a strictly quasi-concave, twice-differentiable utility function. We will, however, make two alternative assumptions about the arguments of the latter. The first assumption considers only leisure (and not work) to be an argument of the social welfare function (i.e., the 'leisure semantic device' is adopted); while the second assumption explicitly includes the uses of manpower in production (tasks) among the arguments of the social welfare function. We will, therefore, make the following two assumptions.

Assumption 2.4(a)   The utility function of society is defined over the set of desired goods. The latter includes k types of leisure, denoted by y_{0k} corresponding to the number of skills available to the economy and n different produced outputs, $y_1, \ldots, y_n$; i.e.,

$$U(y_0, y), \text{ with } U_{y_{0k}} > 0 \text{ for all } k \text{ and } U_{y_i} > 0 \text{ for all } i.$$

Assumption 2.4(b)   The utility function is defined over the set of desired goods and *over the set of the tasks*;[3] i.e.,

$$U(y_0, y, x_1, x_2, \ldots, x_n) \text{ with } U_{y_{0k}} > 0 \text{ for all } k \text{ and}$$

$$U_{y_i} > 0 \text{ for all } i.$$

The meaning of Assumption 2.4(a) is made clearer by the following proposition.

Proposition 2.1   Under A2.1, A2.2, A2.3 and A2.4a (taking the others as given),

(i)   different levels of employment of skill k in production, denoted by L_k, imply different levels of social welfare;

(ii)   different task allocations, which do not change the level of employment of skill k in production, imply the same level of social welfare.

Proof The level of employment of the manpower resource with skill k, L_k, is equal to $\Sigma_i \Sigma_j x_{ij}^k$, where x_{ij}^k is the amount of task j in firm i performed by units of manpower with skill k. Since

$$x_{0k} + \sum_i \sum_j x_{ij}^k = L_k$$

and

$$y_{0k} = x_{0k}$$

then

$$y_{0k} = L_k - \sum_i \sum_j x_{ij}^k.$$

Assuming that both the output level of goods y and the task allocation and employment of the other skills are fixed, then

$$dU = U_{y_{0k}} \, dy_{0k} = -U_{y_{0k}} \sum_i \sum_j dx_{ij}^k.$$

Since $U_{y_{0k}} > 0$, it follows that:

$$\sum_i \sum_j dx_{ij}^k \neq 0 \text{ implies } dU \neq 0 \qquad\qquad (\text{i}')$$

$$\sum_i \sum_j dx_{ij}^k = 0 \text{ implies } dU = 0 \qquad\qquad (\text{ii}')$$

Since (i$'$) implies proposition 2.1(i) and (ii$'$) implies proposition 2.1(ii), we have shown proposition 2.1.

Thus, the use of the 'leisure semantic device' is tantamount to assuming that the total amount of manpower expended in production affects social welfare but that, given the amount, a change in the allocation of manpower among different productive uses does not affect social utility, since in that case the amount of leisure-time is unchanged. Furthermore, we can easily verify that if, following assumption 2.4(b), we explicitly include the tasks performed in production among the arguments of the utility function, proposition 2.1(ii) does not follow except in the particular case in which the members of society are indifferent among the uses of their manpower in production.

Proposition 2.2   Under A2.1, A2.2, A2.3 and A2.4(b), for skill k, different task allocations, which do not change the level of the skill k in production (i.e., L_k), imply different levels of social welfare, except for the particular case in which the marginal social utility of each task is the same.

Proof   Recall that the level of employment of the manpower resource with skill k, L_k is equal to $\Sigma_i\Sigma_j x_{ij}^k$; since the latter is constant, it follows that

$$\sum_i \sum_j dx_{ij}^k = 0.$$

Define a new task allocation $\hat{x}_i$ of the skill, such that: $\hat{x}_{ir} = x_{ir} + dx_{ir}$, $\hat{x}_{is} = x_{is} + dx_{is}$, for some r, s, and $\hat{x}_{ij} = x_{ij}$, for all j, $j \neq r$, $j \neq s$. From (2.1) it follows that $dx_{ir} = -dx_{is}$. From A2.4(b) it follows that

$$dU = U_{x_{ir}} dx_{ir} - U_{x_{is}} dx_{is}$$

which implies that $dU = 0$ for only the particular case in which $U_{x_{ir}} = U_{x_{is}}$.

The resource allocation models, adopting the 'leisure semantic device' (i.e., A2.4(a)), implicitly assume that workers are indifferent towards the different tasks that are performed by a fixed amount of a certain skilled manpower resource. Society is considered to be better off with more consumption goods and more leisure, the latter implying less work-time. The quality of the time spent in work is assumed not to be relevant to social welfare.

3   *First: de-skill jobs*

We have seen that, for the classical economists, the problem of stating how the division of labour was organized and how it should be organized for improving social welfare was a crucial problem in economic analysis. Smith's proposition that market exchange was the cause of the division of labour and the latter was the cause of the wealth of nations could be considered not only as one of the most important causal chains of economic analysis but also as the starting point of the latter. Smith, contradicting his argument that specialization increased (at least job-specific) skills and therefore social welfare, complained about the de-skilling and degrading effects of the division of labour (see chapter 1, section 3.2).

On the other hand, Gioia considered that it is precisely this decrease of the skill (de-skilling) required for producing wealth that is the main advantage of the division of labour (see chapter 1, section 2.1), and for the same reason James Mill maintained that an increase in specialization increases social welfare (chapter 2, section 2.3). Furthermore, Babbage observed that this de-skilling was realized by any 'master-manufacturer' or any profit-maximizing manager because it decreased his costs (chapter 1, sections 2.1 and 3.2).

The 'joint' contribution of Babbage, Gioia and Mill therefore can be considered to lie in the double statement that, in order to maximize social welfare, the division of labour must be organized so as to reduce the skill content of jobs as much as possible, and that this kind of optimal division of labour is introduced spontaneously by each profit-maximizing manager because it coincides with the organization of production that minimizes his costs. Marx criticized the first part of this double statement and disputed the identification of the division of labour within the firm with the optimal or natural division of labour (chapter 3, section 2).

These problems, which were so crucial and so relevant for the classical economist, have occupied the minds of economists much less since the advent of the marginalist revolution. In fact, they have become the subject matter of a separate field, called 'management science'. The starting point of this science can be considered F. Taylor's 'scientific management', which developed in the United States at the turn of this century. As Braverman has described in his excellent book, *Labour and Monopoly Capital* (1974),[4] Taylor pushed the Babbage principle to its extreme consequences, developing more detailed principles by which the division of labour should be organized within an efficient firm.

The effects and extension of the application of Taylorism is still a very debated issue. However, this discussion has usually been conducted outside the boundaries that orthodox economic theory has given to itself. On the other hand, we will show that the 'Gioia–Babbage–Mill double statement', criticized by Marx, is still implicit in the resource allocation models that adopt the leisure device. We will start by defining three concepts which can help us to understand the effects of de-skilling jobs on social welfare.

Definition 3.1   The set of skills $[S_k]$ such that each S_k is capable of being assigned to a job J_α^i will be called the set of employable skills for job J_α^i and will be denoted by E_α^i.

For example, referring to definition 2.2, under organization of production (ii), we have that E_1^i is $[S_1, S_2, S_3]$, and E_2^i is $[S_1, S_4]$.

Definition 3.2 The cardinality of a job J_α^i, denoted by (J_α^i), is the number of tasks to be performed in the job J_α^i.

Definition 3.3 A change in the organization of production of firm i is called de-skilling if the cardinality of at least one of the jobs decreases, without increasing the cardinality of any other job in the organization, and if the new organization of production satisfies the condition that the set of jobs $[J_\alpha^i]$ includes the set of tasks X_i.

For example, for firm i, a change in the organization of production from (i) to (ii) of definition 2.2 would be de-skilling. Also, a change from an organization defined by $J_1 = [x_1, x_2]$, $J_2 = [x_2, x_3]$, $J_3 = [x_4]$ to one defined by $J_1' = [x_1]$, $J_2' = [x_2, x_3]$, $J_3' = [x_4]$ would be called de-skilling.

We can now argue that resource allocation models bring about conclusions rather more extreme than the ones put forward by James Mill. In the framework of resource allocation models, de-skilling is essentially a way of relaxing the skill constraints in an economy by enlarging the set of employable skills. This allows a greater (or at least the same) level of social welfare to be achieved with *given* endowments of skilled manpower, the latter circumstance occurring independently of the savings on training time.

More precisely, we can state the following proposition.

Proposition 3.1 Under A2.1, A2.2, A2.3 and A2.4(a), de-skilling either leaves unchanged or increases social welfare.

Proof Since each output vector that was feasible before de-skilling is still feasible after de-skilling, proposition 3.1 follows.

Consider the following example:

(i)   there is one firm in the economy producing output y;
(ii) the set of tasks to be performed in the firm is (x_1, x_2, x_3); i.e., $y = f(x_1, x_2, x_3)$;
(iii) there are four skills available through the manpower resource:
S_1 is able to perform $[x_{01}, x_1, x_2, x_3]$;
S_2 is able to perform $[x_{02}, x_1, x_2]$;
S_3 is able to perform $[x_{03}, x_2, x_3]$;
S_4 is able to perform $[x_{04}, x_1]$;

(iv)   case A' there exist two jobs, J_{1A}, J_{2A}, in the firm, defined
       by the sets of tasks $[x_1, x_2]$ and $[x_2, x_3]$, respectively;
(v)   case B: there exist two jobs, J_{1B}, J_{2B}, in the firm, defined
       by the set of tasks $[x_1]$, $[x_2, x_3]$, respectively.

The problem is, then, to maximize social welfare under the two
cases, given the data in (i)–(v).

For case A, the problem can be written as follows:

$$\max U(y_0, y)$$

subject to: $y = f(x_1, x_2, x_3)$

$$y_{0k} = x_{0k}, \qquad k = 1, \ldots, 4$$

$$x_1 \in E_{1A}, \qquad \text{where } E_{1A} = [S_1, S_2]$$

$$x_2 \in E_{1A}$$

$$x_2 \in E_{2A}, \qquad \text{where } E_{2A} = [S_1, S_3]$$

$$x_3 \in E_{2A}$$

$$x_{0k} + \sum_j x_j^k = L_k \quad k = 1, \ldots, 4.$$

For case B, we have:

$$\max U(y_0, y)$$

subject to: $y = f(x_1, x_2, x_3)$

$$y_{0k} = x_{0k}, \qquad k = 1, \ldots, 4$$

$$x_1 \in E_{1B}, \qquad \text{where } E_{1B} = [S_1, S_2, S_4]$$

$$x_2 \in E_{2B}, \qquad \text{where } E_{2B} = [S_1, S_3]$$

$$x_3 \in E_{2B}$$

$$x_{0k} + \sum_j x_j^k = L_k \quad k = 1, \ldots, 4.$$

The change in organization from case A to case B clearly
represents de-skilling. Hence, if we show that each solution for
case A is feasible for case B (whereas the contrary does not hold),
then we have shown for this example that de-skilling either
increases or leaves unchanged social welfare.

The feasibility of a solution to A under case B can be seen as
follows. The allocation $[\hat{x}_0, \hat{x}]$ corresponding to an optimal

solution $\hat{y}$ in A is feasible in case B since

$$\hat{x}_1 \in E_{1B} \text{ for } \hat{x}_1 \in E_{1A} \subset E_{1B}$$

$$\hat{x}_2 \in E_{1B} \text{ for } \hat{x}_2 \in E_{1A} \subset E_{1B}$$

$$\hat{x}_2 \in E_{2B} \text{ for } \hat{x}_2 \in E_{2A} = E_{2B}$$

$$\hat{x}_3 \in E_{2B} \text{ for } \hat{x}_3 \in E_{2A} = E_{2B}$$

and satisfies the resource constraints.

On the other hand, for the same reason job de-skilling also either increases or at worst leaves unchanged the profits of a 'master-manufacturer' who produces a certain output vector by employing some given amounts of skilled resources. Since each output vector that was possible before de-skilling is still feasible after de-skilling (while new output vectors may be feasible), de-skilling can only increase profits, or leave them unchanged.

Thus, the conclusion that can be derived from the resource allocation model is that the internal allocation of manpower will be organized by a profit-maximizing manager according to the criterion that the de-skilling of jobs is never disadvantageous and that such an organization of manpower is consistent with the aim of improving social welfare.

This result is, of course, based on the supposition implicit in resource allocation models, that it is manpower units converted into leisure, and not into work, that affects utility. We can immediately see that, when preferences about the allocation of work are properly taken into account, the opposite result may occur.

Proposition 3.2   Under A2.1, A2.2, A2.3 and A2.4(b), de-skilling may decrease social welfare.

Proof   It follows immediately from proposition 2.2 that, since de-skilling implies a change in relative task levels for at least one of the skills employed in production, a decrease in social welfare may occur.

Thus, de-skilling jobs may decrease social welfare even though it may increase profits, and may imply that new output vectors, which are preferred by society, are produced. The latter circumstance is likely to occur when the reduction of a job to the single repetition of the same task worsens the quality of working life. This could easily happen if we consider the old assumption of Jevons that the marginal disutility of performing a specific task increases after a certain point.[5]

4 Second: be efficient

We have just seen that, if the 'leisure semantic device' is adopted, the suggestions of the 'advocates' of scientific management lead to improvements of social welfare, whatever the preferences of society. This implies that, according to mainstream economic theory, a manager of a firm or the 'central planner' of a 'single-firm society' is allowed, from the point of view of welfare economics, to dictate important aspects of working life following a simple rule: namely, de-skill jobs, whenever this is possible. The idea that production can be 'efficiently' organized without taking into account the preferences of workers but in such a way as to be consistent with their preferences is deeply rooted in resource allocation models.[6] The aim of this section is to show how this idea is again based on the fact that in the orthodox approach it is manpower units converted into leisure and not work that is supposed to affect utility.

Let us first outline the traditional line of reasoning. Because of the non-satiation assumption (i.e., $U_{y_i} > 0$ for all i and $U_{y_{0k}} > 0$ for all k; or additional amounts of desired goods, including leisure, yield greater utility), it is clear that the greater the attainable output (y_0, y), the higher is the level of social welfare. Therefore, if we define an efficient output vector (y_0, y) to be a feasible set of outputs, such that an increase in one of the components can be achieved only by a decrease in some other component, it follows that efficiency is a necessary condition for social welfare maximization.

We can see how this condition permits the solution to the optimization problem to be carried out in two independent steps. The first step is to find the set of efficient output vectors from the feasible set, while the second is to determine which efficient output vector maximizes social welfare.

Let us consider the first step in greater detail. In order to solve for the set of efficient output vectors it is not necessary to consider preferences. Preferences are necessary only in order to determine which efficient output vector should be produced. For example, given a quantity of the resource, manpower, each manager of a firm can calculate, independently of any information on social preferences, which level of task allocation, x_i, gives rise to maximum attainable output. That is, the quantity of manpower is allocated among productive uses in such a way that it is not possible to increase output further. This is tantamount to saying that, given a set of inputs, the manager of a firm is able to choose a technique of production entirely through the pure technological relationship between inputs and outputs; or, in our case, the criterion upon which a manager can choose the level of tasks to be performed by the available manpower allocation is independent of price or social preference information. For the same reasons, a central planner of a single-firm economy could choose the technological relationships and the organization of production that is necessary in order to maximize social welfare without taking into account the preferences of members of society.

These results of orthodox economics are, however, based on the assumption that work is a variable that enters only the production function and that influences utility only indirectly (i.e., on assumption 2.4(a)). If we assume that the uses of manpower in production affect social welfare (i.e., assumption 2.4(b)), then the following proposition can be stated.

Proposition 4.1 Under A2.1, A2.2, A2.3 and A2.4(b), if an output vector $\hat{y}$ is such that $\hat{y} - y > 0$, then it is not necessary for the social welfare level associated with $\hat{y}$ to be greater than the level of social welfare associated with y.

Proof Define the inverse function $f_{ij}^{-1}(y_i; \bar{x}_{i)j(})$ for task x_{ij}, $j = 1, \ldots, T$. Consider an output vector $\hat{y}$ and output vector y, such that for good 1 $\hat{y}_1 - y_1 > 0$, and for all the other goods $\hat{y}_i = y_i$. Set

$$d\hat{y}_1 = \hat{y}_1 - y_1 > 0.$$

Then

$$dU = U_{y_1}\, d\hat{y}_1 + \sum_j U_{x_{ij}} \frac{\partial f_{ij}^{-1}}{\partial y_1}\, d\hat{y}_1.$$

Since the second term of the right-hand side of this equality may be negative, it follows that an increase in output may decrease social welfare.

An immediate corollary of proposition 4.1 is as follows.

Proposition 4.2 Under A2.1, A2.2, A2.3 and A2.4(b), efficiency of the output vector is no longer a necessary condition for maximum social welfare.

Thus, when preferences about work are properly taken into account, the problem of maximizing social welfare cannot usefully be broken into two steps, the first of which is independent of information concerning social welfare. The problem of choosing the set of optimal techniques of production cannot be treated purely as an engineering problem. Social preferences matter not only in order to determine which output vector should be produced, but also in order to decide how (i.e., by the use of which techniques) output should be produced. The use of a certain technique involves a certain set of uses of manpower to which society cannot be indifferent. A member of society may prefer less output to be produced if this implies a more enjoyable quality of working life. Technological efficiency can be a misleading concept; 'more efficiency' could decrease social welfare, and therefore could mean 'more *in*efficiency' when the preferences of society are taken into account.

Central planners and managers, who in the traditional approach could argue that they can dictate *how* work should be organized and allocated (since in the traditional approach preferences matter only in order to decide what and how much to produce), cannot justify their allocative power under the (holy) name of efficiency when the fact that work influences utility is properly considered.

Furthermore, we can easily see that 'the profit-maximizing rule' is equivalent to the 'technological efficiency rule', since an increase in efficiency (i.e., of the output vector that is obtained with a given amount of manpower) increases the profits of a manager who is allocating a given amount of manpower within his firm. Therefore, as for the case of an efficient allocation, the allocation of a certain amount of manpower which is realized by a profit-maximizing manager inside his firm can be incompatible with the aim of maximizing social welfare when this objective is assumed to depend in addition on the uses of manpower in production.

5   Third: profit-maximize

We have seen in the two preceding sections that profit-maximizing behaviour can bring about allocations of manpower within the firm that are inconsistent with the aim of maximizing social welfare. A well-known result of resource allocation models is that a social optimum can be 'decentralized' to the profit-maximizing managers and to a 'distributor', the latter being a collective consumer who knows the social welfare function.

In order to re-examine these fundamental results of mainstream economics, the analysis will be simplified by making the following assumption.

Assumption 5.1 Assume that there is only one skill associated with the available manpower resource in the economy, and that this skill S is capable of performing the complete set of tasks X. If there are L units of available manpower, the resource constraint for this model would then be:

$$x_0 + \sum_i \sum_j x_{ij} = L.$$

We can thus re-assess, in the language of our model, the decentralization properties of the resource allocation models.

Proportion 5.1 Under A2.1, A5.1, A2.3 and A2.4(a), it is possible to decentralize a social optimum to a distributor, who knows the social welfare function $U(y_0, y)$, and to the profit-maximizing managers of n firms, provided that there exists a set of shadow prices $\lambda_0, \lambda_1, \ldots, \lambda_n, \lambda_R$, one for each output (including leisure) and one for manpower.

Proof In order to maximize $U(y_0, y)$ subject to:

$$y_0 = x_0$$
$$y_i = f_i(x_i) \text{ for all } i$$
$$x_0 + \sum_i \sum_j x_{ij} = L$$

we form the Lagrangean function

$$L(y_0, y, \ldots, x_n, \lambda) = U(y_0, y) - \sum_i \lambda_i \{y_i - f_i(x_i)\}$$
$$- \lambda_0(y_0 - x_0) - \lambda_R\left(x_0 + \sum_i \sum_j x_{ij} - L\right).$$

The necessary first-order conditions are:

$$U_{y_i} \leqslant \lambda_i \tag{5.1}$$
$$U_{y_0} \leqslant \lambda_0 \tag{5.2}$$

$$\lambda_i \frac{\partial f_i}{\partial x_{ij}} \leqslant \lambda_R \quad i = 1, \ldots, n, \quad j = 1, \ldots, T \tag{5.3}$$

$$\lambda_0 \leqslant \lambda_R . \tag{5.4}$$

From (5.2) and (5.4),

$$U_{y_0} \leqslant \lambda_R . \tag{5.5}$$

The distributor maximizes the difference between utility and costs; i.e.,

$$U(y_0, y) - \sum_i \lambda_i y_i - \lambda_R y_0$$

which yields the following first-order necessary conditions:

$$U_{y_i}^i \leqslant \lambda_i \quad i = 1, \ldots, n \tag{5.1'}$$

$$U_{y_0} \leqslant \lambda_R . \tag{5.5'}$$

For each i, firm i maximizes

$$\pi_i = \lambda_i y_i - \lambda_R \sum_j x_{ij}$$

which yields the first-order necessary conditions:

$$\lambda_i \frac{\partial f_i}{\partial x_{ij}} \leqslant \lambda_R . \tag{5.3'}$$

Proposition 5.1 is shown by the equivalence of (5.1), (5.3) and (5.5) to (5.1'), (5.3') and (5.5').

Thus, if we interpret the shadow prices as market equilibrium prices,[7] proposition 5.1 implies that, for each firm, only one price and one market transaction are necessary in order to achieve the best allocation of manpower among different uses. However, this circumstance arises from the fact that, when workers are assumed to be indifferent about the allocation of their manpower, the internal allocation of a profit-maximizing manager is consistent with the conditions that are necessary for maximizing social welfare. The latter conditions (i.e., (5.3)) imply, if we exclude corner solutions, that the marginal productivity of manpower should be the same in each productive use; i.e.,

$$\frac{\partial f_i}{\partial x_{i1}} = \frac{\partial f_i}{\partial x_{i2}} = \ldots = \frac{\partial f_i}{\partial x_{iT}} . \tag{5.6}$$

The same conditions are realized by a manager who allocates a certain endowment of manpower within a firm i in such a way that profits are maximized. The latter will in fact maximize $\lambda_i y_i$ subject to $\Sigma_j x_{ij} = \bar{L}_i$, the optimum necessary conditions being again condition (5.6).

Thus, the market has only to take account of the fact that manpower must be distributed among the different firms in the right proportion. The optimal distribution of manpower among different uses within each firm can be left to the profit-maximizing managers.

However, these results are limited to the case in which workers are (implicitly) assumed to be indifferent among the uses of their own manpower. When the preferences of society about the use of their work are appropriately taken into account, the optimization problem that is faced by society should be rewritten in the following way:

$$\max U(y_0, y, x_1, \ldots, x_n)$$

$$\text{subject to } y_0 = x_0$$

$$y_i = f_i(x_i)$$

$$x_0 + \sum_i \sum_j x_{ij} = L.$$

In this case the first-order necessary conditions are:

$$U_{y_i} \leqslant \lambda_i \quad i = 1, \ldots, n \tag{5.1'}$$

$$U_{y_0} \leqslant \lambda_0 \tag{5.2'}$$

$$U_{x_{ij}} + \lambda_i f^i_{x_{ij}} \leqslant \lambda_R \quad i = 1, \ldots, n, \quad j = 1, \ldots, T \tag{5.3'}$$

$$\lambda_0 \leqslant \lambda_R. \tag{5.4'}$$

From (5.2') and (5.4'),

$$U_{y_0} \leqslant \lambda_R. \tag{5.5'}$$

Condition (5.3') implies that the *sum* of the marginal productivity (in value) and the marginal utility of work should be equal in each use; i.e., excluding corner solutions, for all i,

$$U_{x_{i1}} + \lambda_i f^i_{x_{i1}} = U_{x_{i2}} + \lambda_i f^i_{x_{i2}} = \ldots = U_{x_{iT}} + \lambda_i f^i_{x_{iT}} \tag{5.7}$$

The interpretation of condition (5.7) is as follows. When the preferences of members of society about the allocation of work are appropriately represented in the social welfare function, the allocation of manpower, which maximizes social welfare, must be such that not only the marginal productivity but also the marginal (dis)utility of each use of the latter is taken into account.

Since, because of (5.1'), $\lambda_i f^i_{x_{ij}}$ is equal to $U_{y_i}(\partial y_i / \partial x_{ij})$, condition (5.7) means that a necessary condition for optimality is that the *sum* of the *direct* marginal utility (i.e., $U_{x_{ij}}$) and *indirect* marginal utility (i.e., $U_{y_i}(\partial y_i / \partial x_{ij})$) should be the same in each use of manpower.

Condition (5.6) can be considered a particular case of condition (5.7), arising when the *direct* marginal utility of manpower is the same in each use (i.e., when society is indifferent among the uses of manpower). In the latter case only the *indirect* marginal utility (i.e., $U_{y_i}(\partial y_i / \partial x_{ij})$) matters for determining the optimality conditions. In the more general and realistic case (i.e., when preferences about work do matter), condition (5.6), which is obtained by a profit-maximizing manager who allocates manpower inside his firm, fails to be equivalent to the optimum necessary condition (5.7). This suggests that the decentralization properties of resource allocation models should be reformulated, as is confirmed by the following proposition.

Proposition 5.2 Under A2.1, A5.1, A2.3 and A2.4(b), it is possible to decentralize a social optimum to a distributor, who knows the social welfare function, and to the profit-maximizing managers of n firms, provided that there exists a set of shadow prices $\lambda_0, \lambda_1, \ldots, \lambda_n, w_{ij}$ ($i = 1, \ldots, n, j = 1, \ldots, T$), one for each output and one for each task performed in production.

Proof   Let us define task prices w_{ij} such that,

$$\text{for } x_{ij} > 0, \quad \lambda_i f^i_{x_{ij}} = w_{ij} = \lambda_R - U_{x_{ij}}. \tag{5.8}$$

The distributor will

$$\max U(y_0, y, x_1, \ldots, x_n) - \sum_i \lambda_i y_i$$

$$- \lambda_R(y_0 - x_0) + \sum_i \sum_j w_{ij} x_{ij} \tag{5.9}$$

$$\text{subject to } x_0 + \sum_i \sum_j x_{ij} = L. \tag{5.10}$$

Substituting (5.10) into (5.9), we obtain the following first-order necessary conditions for the distributor:

$$U_{y_i} \leqslant \lambda_i \quad i = 1, \ldots, n \qquad\qquad (5.1'')$$

$$U_{y_0} \leqslant \lambda_R \qquad\qquad (5.2'')$$

$$U_{x_{ij}} + w_{ij} \leqslant \lambda_R \quad i = 1, \ldots, n, \quad j = 1, \ldots, T. \qquad (5.3'')$$

(5.1″) and (5.2″) are equivalent to (5.1′) and (5.2′); the equivalence of (5.3″) to (5.3′) is obvious if we refer to (5.8).

The firm i will maximize profits:

$$\pi_i = \lambda_i y_i - \sum_i \sum_j w_{ij} x_{ij} \quad i = 1, \ldots, n, \quad j = 1, \ldots, T.$$

The firm's optimum conditions are

$$\lambda_i y^i_{x_{ij}} \leqslant w_{ij} \quad j = i, \ldots, T$$

which can be rewritten, because of (5.8), as

$$\text{for } x_{ij} > 0, \quad \lambda_i y^i_{x_{ij}} = \lambda_R - U_{x_{ij}}. \qquad (5.3''')$$

Since (5.3‴) is equivalent to (5.3′), the firms, too, realize a social optimum.

We can interpret the prices w_{ij} either as market equilibrium prices or as shadow prices which are implicit in the optimal allocation calculated by a planning office and issued by it to the profit-maximizing managers.[8]

If we interpret the prices w_{ij} as market equilibrium prices, proposition 5.2 implies that $n \times T$ prices and $n \times T$ transactions[9] are necessary in order to achieve the best allocation of manpower among different uses. So many market transactions are required by the fact that, when the social welfare function includes the uses of manpower among its arguments, the internal allocation of profit-maximizing managers would be inconsistent with the social welfare optimum conditions. In the latter case, therefore, the allocative power of profit-maximizing managers over labour is unjustified; each allocation of the latter should be the object of market transactions and should be contracted in the market. Only this method of allocation is successful in meeting the social welfare optimum conditions that managers would otherwise fail to achieve inside their firms.

6   *The authoritarian implications of orthodox economics*

The authoritarian content of the rules that can be deduced when the leisure device is adopted is indeed striking. The first rule (i.e., de-skill jobs) restates Mill's idea that the division of labour should be organized in such a way that each job contains the minimum possible number of tasks. According to this rule, jobs should be designed in such a way that some tasks (and in particular the ones requiring a higher level of skill) are separated from the rest. In this way a hierarchy of jobs is created; at the bottom we have the most simple and repetitive tasks, and at the top we have the jobs constituted by more skilled and creative tasks. The separation of the more complex from the more simple tasks also implies, as a particular case, the separation of the ideation and direction tasks from the (simpler) execution tasks. The authoritarian implications of this separation are evident. The divisions of labour that a profit-maximizing manager introduces would follow this de-skilling rule. It would therefore be perfectly consistent with this implicit suggestion of welfare economics and with the explicit suggestion of F. Taylor.

As to the second rule (i.e., improve technological efficiency or maximize output), its authoritarian content is also apparent. It implies that the allocation of work can be decided by considering pure technological relationships between inputs and outputs, quite independently of the preferences of the workers. Moreover, it is not hard to find in it that kind of product fetishism that Marx observed characterized the works of the political economics of his age. Finally, this is a rule that would be realized by a profit-maximizing manager who allocates a given amount of manpower within his firm.

We can now turn to the third rule (i.e., allocate labour within the firm by profit-maximizing), which implies that the decisions concerning the organization of production can be left to managers who buy manpower at its market equilibrium price and allocate it in the firm among the various production tasks in such a way that profits are maximized. The authority of the managers who decide which tasks the workers will perform should be respected by the workers, because the allocation of work that maximizes profits also maximizes social welfare.

The authoritarian content of this rule does not even need to be commented upon; indeed, we have already seen how, like the other two rules, it relies on the assumption that members of society derive utility only from the products of their work (including leisure) and therefore have nothing to say about the organization of work as such. When the preferences of workers for the allocation of their own work are taken into account, the organization of work cannot be left to the internal allocation of the profit-maximizing managers. In this case, either a central planning office (which maximizes the social welfare that the individuals derive both from their work and from the products of their work) or a 'complete' market system (where a market and a price exists for each single task) is required for maximizing social welfare.

These conclusions are, however, obtained under a very restrictive assumption which we are going to remove in the following chapters: that there are no costs involved in using either the market or the planning system.

Notes

1   Arrow and Hahn (1971) generalize the semantic device to more than one skill; Arrow and Hurwicz (1960), Malinvaud (1967), Kornai and Liptak (1963) and Heal (1973) directly assume that all the outputs are positively desired and that inputs are not negatively desired.

2   These rules are implied by profit maximization when labour is allocated *within* the firm according to this criterion (without the existence of a separate market contract for each task).

3   Since each firm i stands for a firm of 'type i', we assume in A2.4(b) that members of society have preferences not only for the tasks *per se* but also for the 'type' of firm in which the task is performed. For instance, the location of the firm and, in general the working environment can be considered as characteristics that define the 'type' of firm and to which the workers are unlikely to be indifferent. By contrast, the fact that we consider only one representative firm for each type of firm implies that members of society are indifferent to firms of the same type. The focus of our analysis will, however, be about the preferences of society for tasks *per se.*

4   The impact of job de-skilling, and a discussion of the application of Taylorism to production processes, is very well presented in Braverman (1974). For the relationship of Braverman's work with orthodox Marxism and neoclassical theory, see Pagano (1978a). On job routinization, see Fritzroy (1978); also, Marglin (1974) and Cohen (1981).

5   See Jevons (1970, chapter V) and section 2 of chapter 5 above.

6   For a very lucid criticism of the concept of technological efficiency, see Sen (1975).

7   The interpretation of the shadow prices as market equilibrium requires that the firms are price-takers. This interpretation is possible if we recall that 'firm i' could be interpreted as meaning 'many firms of type i', and therefore if we assume that many firms produce the same product. An alternative interpretation of the shadow prices can be given by

imagining that they are calculated by a planning office which solves the optimization problem for society as a whole and issues the prices to the firms and the distributor. This meaning of 'shadow prices' is going to be more closely investigated in the following chapter, where we will see how shadow prices can be calculated by the planning office without having to solve the whole optimization problem.

8 See n. 7 above.

9 The prices should be $n \times T$. However, if workers are only interested in task *per se* (see n. 3 above), only T task prices would be necessary. In both cases, the number of transactions required by the market would be $n \times T$ (i.e., T transactions for each firm).

8

Planning markets and firms

Introduction

In the preceding chapter, we arrived at the somewhat extreme conclusion that either a centrally planned economy (where the arguments of the planner's objective function include tasks) or a market economy (where all products and all tasks are traded at market equilibrium prices) can achieve the aim of realizing an optimum allocation of resources; by contrast, if managers try to allocate manpower within their own firms by choosing the pattern of work allocation that maximizes profits, they will fail to achieve an optimum allocation of resources.

Managers can realize an optimum allocation of resources either by implementing an optimal allocation that has been calculated by some (omniscient) central planning office, or by maximizing profits and making a market contract for each task to be performed. In both cases, we can say that no sub-unit of an economy endowed with autonomous allocative power on labour-power exists; or, as will become clear in the following pages, no *firm* exists in the economy.

However, such extreme conclusions were arrived at in the preceding chapter under the very unrealistic assumption that there are no costs of using either planning system or the market system. This chapter examines two distinct but converging streams of the literature written on this topic during present century. The first considers the costs of using the planning system and comes to the conclusion that some decisions should be decentralized to firms. The second stream considers the costs of using market transactions and comes to the conclusion that some of these transactions should be internalized within organizations as firms. Though starting from different points, both streams of the literature can be used to justify the existence of firms from the point of view of welfare economics.

138

1 *Decentralizing decisions to the firms*

In his paper, 'Economic Calculation in the Socialist Common-wealth', the Austrian economist L. von Mises maintained that 'Socialism is the abolition of rational economy.' 'Where there is no free market,' he wrote, 'there is no economic calculation' (Mises, 1920, pp. 80, 81).

We have seen that, in a certain sense, an anticipatory response to von Mises's statement was already contained in the work of another Austrian economist, von Wieser (see chapter 5, section 4). Wieser had shown how prices can be calculated independently of actual market exchange. Therefore, if prices were necessary in order to have a rational economy, in theory they could be calculated even if a free market did not exist.

Before the publication of Mises's article, the insights of Wieser had already been developed further by Pareto in his *Cours d'économie politique* (1896) and more completely by Barone in his paper, 'Il Ministro Della Produzione nello stato collettivista', first published in 1908 in the *Giornale degli Economisti.* The starting point of Barone and Pareto is the Walrasian system. We saw in chapter 6 that Walras had shown how it was possible to determine the prices and quantities exchanged and produced under the conditions of a competitive equilibrium, on the basis of certain data including consumer preferences, the state of the technology and an initial distribution of resource endowments. Moreover, he had also shown that, under certain conditions, the competitive solution was equivalent to that allocation of resources which maximized economic welfare. It followed from this double statement that a centrally planned socialist economy should replicate the solution of the Walrasian system if its aim was to maximize social welfare.

This consequence of the Walrasian approach was explicitly put forward by Pareto and Barone. In particular, Barone maintained that, if the data of the Walrasian system were known by the Ministry of Production of a collectivist state, then it would be possible for this state to find a rational – and, indeed, optimal – solution to the planning problem by solving the equations of the Walrasian system. The equivalence between the market solution and the solution under the planned regime demonstrated to Barone 'how fantastic those doctrines are which imagine that production in the collectivist regime would be ordered in a manner substantially different from that of anarchist production' (1908, p. 73). By contrast, he points out,

> [if] the Ministry of Production proposes to obtain the collective maximum – which it obviously must, whatever law of distribution may be adopted – all the economist categories of the old regime must reappear, though may be with other names: prices, salaries, rent, profit, saving, etc. Not only that: but, always provided that it wishes to obtain that maximum with the services of which the individuals and the community dispose, the same two fundamental conditions which characterize free competition reappear, and the maximum is more nearly attained the more perfectly they are realized. We refer, of course, to the conditions of minimum cost of production and the equalization of price to cost of production. (Barone, 1908, p. 73)

The collectivist regime can therefore be seen as a particular case of the individualistic regime:

> to hand over some capital to the State and afterwards to distribute the yield thereof among the individuals, according to a certain law, whatever it is, is like starting from a situation in the individualist regime, in which the individuals, besides having their own capital, may be possessors of certain quotas of capital of which the State has become the controller, quotas corresponding to that same of distribution which we supposed adopted. (Barone, 1908, p. 73)

In spite of the fact that this argument implies the theoretical feasibility of rational economic calculation under a collectivist regime, Barone indicates a difficulty of centralized planning that makes it either unfeasible or at least extremely costly. He believes that the economic variability of technical coefficients makes their determination practically impossible for the Minister of Production of a collectivist state. Even if this determination were possible, a costly 'army of officials whose services would be devoted not to production but to the laborious and colossal centralisation work of the Ministry' (p. 74) necessary for organizing production under a collectivist regime.

The costs of economic planning were pointed out more clearly by Hayek. Referring to the application of the Walrasian system to the solution of the planning problem, he maintained that 'this is not an impossibility in the sense that it is logically contradictory .... But to argue that a determination of prices by such a procedure being logically conceivable in any way invalidates the contention that it is not a possible solution, only proves that the real nature of the problem has not been perceived.' Hayek agrees that 'any such solution would have to be based on the solution of some such system of equations as that developed in Barone's article.' 'But,' he argues, 'what is practically relevant here is not the formal structure of this system, but the nature and amount of concrete information required if a numerical solution is to be attempted, and the magnitude of the task which this numerical solution must involve in any modern community' (Hayek, 1935, pp. 207, 208).

Hayek describes the enormity of the volume of information that would have to be collected by a planning authority in order to solve the system of equations described by Barone. In a centrally planned economy, central direction takes the place of the initiative of the manager of the individual enterprise. Such central direction will have to include, and be intimately responsible for, details of the most minute description. He observes:

> It is impossible to decide rationally how much material or new machinery should be assigned to any one enterprise and at what price (in an accounting sense) it will be rational to do so, without also deciding at the same time whether and in which way the machinery and tools already in use should continue to be used or be disposed of. (Hayek, 1935, p. 208)

A central plan that is not to be hopelessly wasteful must therefore take into account such details of technique, and must necessarily treat machinery of the same type but in different locations and different conditions as different goods. Since in a centrally planned economy 'the manager of the individual plant would be deprived of the discretion of substituting at will one kind of commodity, all this immense mass of different units would necessarily have to enter separately into the calculations of the planning authority' (p. 209). This concentration of information regarding the single plant is obviously not feasible, Hayek feels. Moreover, this problem leads to another, to which he attributes even greater importance. 'The usual theoretical abstractions used in the explanation of equilibrium in a competitive system includes the assumption that a certain range of technical knowledge is given' (p. 210). But this technical knowledge is usually dispersed among many people. It follows that, in a centrally planned economy, the selection of the most appropriate technique involves not only the collection and concentration of all the data regarding individual plants, but also the concentration of the technical knowledge needed to use these data efficiently; and 'It is probably evident that the mere assembly of these data is a task beyond human capacity' (p. 211).

However, even if this difficulty could be overcome, the planning procedure would have completed only the first of the two steps that are necessary to find a solution to the planning problem. It is still necessary to calculate the unknown quantities that we need to know on the basis of these data. The large number of unknowns involved may well imply that a lifetime is necessary to solve this mathematical problem.

Neither the collection of this information nor the performance of these calculations is necessary in a market economy, where market prices are cheap and efficient transmitters of information. Prices embody sufficient information for the individual agent's decision nexus. In a planned economy, by contrast, the collection and processing of information through a central body uses up scarce resources.

Lange's (1936) model of a socialist society[1] was intended to overcome Hayek's objections. In his model, a market exists for consumption goods and labour while the planning of production activities is organized in such a way that production decisions are decentralized to firms. Although there is an important difference, as we will see in the following pages, we can say that the planning office of Lange's socialist society works much like the Walrasian auctioneer and is intended to imitate the market mechanism. Lange explicitly points out that the planning office can formulate the plan 'by a method of trial and error similar to that in a competitive market'. He assumes that the central planning board starts with a given set of prices chosen at random. However, he points out that in a real-life situation the task would be easier, since the planning office would proceed with prices historically given; in that case, much smaller adjustments would be necessary since 'there would be no necessity of building up an entirely new price system' (p. 33).

In Lange's model, 'All decisions of the managers of production and of productive resources in public ownership and also all decisions of individuals as consumers and suppliers of labour are made on the basis of these prices [initially chosen at random]. ... As a result of these decisions the quantity demanded and supplied of each commodity is determined' (p. 33). The central planning board then increases (decreases) the prices of each commodity for which there is an excess demand (supply). Such a procedure is repeated several times until a set of equilibrium prices is finally determined. 'Thus,' Lange maintained, 'the accounting prices in a socialist economy can be determined by the same process of trial and error by which prices on a competitive market are determined' (p. 33). In order to determine these prices, the planning office does not need to collect any information about firms' technologies, nor does it need the technical knowledge required to make an efficient use of this information. Moreover, no complicated calculation is necessary at central level. The individual units have only 'to calculate' the quantities that optimize their objective functions, as they do in a market economy. In Lange's model, the planning office only needs information about the excess demands of each commodity and then simply needs to change prices according to the signs of excess demands – the latter being the only 'calculation' required by the planning procedure.

Thus, the higher and unfeasible costs of centralized planning, pointed out by Hayek, led Lange to propose a model of decentralized planning. In his model, the role of the planning office resembles the role of the Walrasian auctioneer and is intended to perform (better) the role of the market mechanism. In this framework, market and decentralized planning appear to be equivalent forms of organization, both of which could be represented by the Walrasian ticket economy.

The claim of an equivalence of organizational form between a decentralized planned economy and a market economy is fascinating and provocative, but at the same time somewhat misleading. According to Marx (and this point of view has been restated by Dobb, 1933, 1935, and Kornai, 1971, 1973), planning was characterized by an *a priori* coordination of economic activity (see chapter 3, section 1.2). In a planned economy, a single decision is implemented only when the compatibility of the entire set of decisions is ensured. On the contrary, the market coordination of economic activity is characterized by the fact that exchange and production decisions are enacted before such *a priori* and *ex ante* coordination is ensured. We have already seen how this aspect is obscured by approximating the market economy to the auctioneer economy, and we know Walras himself (unlike other modern economists) was at least partially aware of this problem (see chapter 6, section 3). In the auctioneer economy, economic activity is coordinated *ex ante*; agents' intentions, not acts, are communicated to the auctioneer, and no intention is realized before equilibrium prices are reached. By contrast, in a market economy, agents do not communicate their production and exchange decisions to a central agency. Trading and production occur despite the possibility of overall incompatibility between the decisions of the agents. To have approximated the *ex post* coordination mechanism of the market by the *ex ante* coordination mechanism of the auctioneer economy has therefore considerably obscured an essential institutional element that distinguishes the market economy from the planning system. Whereas the market provides an *ex post* coordination of economic activities, planning, like the Walrasian auctioneer, attempts to coordinate activities *ex ante*.

The similarity between a planned economy and the auctioneer economy (and the distinction between it and a market economy) is strongly reinforced by noting that the planning model is perfectly compatible with the existence of a price-setting agency (i.e., the planning office) such as the auctioneer. The market has no institution to assume this role, despite the fact, pointed out by Arrow, that 'the standard development of behaviour under competitive conditions has made both sides of any market take prices as given from some outside agency' (1959, p. 381).

How can price-taking behaviour be reconciled with the absence of a central body? If all the agents are price-takers, who is left to set prices? Clearly, this point is not problematic if the prevailing prices clear markets. But if disequilibrium exists on a market, the absence of a price-adjusting agency will imply that monopolistic price-setting forces must be operative in order for prices to change. Consider the following example. Suppose that the usual assumptions for perfect competitive conditions hold for a market, but that at the prevailing price demand exceeds supply. Furthermore, assume that no firm can increase supply in the short period. Because supply is constrained, any individual entrepreneur perceives that he can raise prices, even if his competitors do not. Thus, the entrepreneur faces a sloping demand curve, and prices change because of monopolistic price-setting behaviour. (On this matter, see Arrow, 1959.)

If we interpret the auctioneer model as a planning model, then Lange's decentralized model of planning shares only some of its characteristics. One common feature of Lange's model and the Walrasian ticket economy is that, in both, there is a price-setting agency. By contrast, the auctioneer–planner of the Walrasian perfect society and Lange's planner adjust prices in a different way. The auctioneer–planner first eliminates all the excess demands and supplies and makes all decisions compatible, and only afterwards allows the agents to implement their decisions. According to the Marxian definition of planning, the auctioneer–planner is therefore a 'true planner', since she coordinates *a priori* the decisions of the agents. Lange's planner acts in a different way. He changes prices whenever an excess of demand or supply exists in the real economy and lets his agents implement their decisions during the adjustment process. According to the definition of Marx, Lange's planner is therefore not a true planner, since he makes no attempt to coordinate *a priori* the decisions of the agents (see chapter 6, section 1.2). Lange's planner and the market mechanism both serve to coordinate the decisions of the agents *a posteriori* – a characteristic that differentiates these two models from the auctioneer–planner model.

This characteristic of the Lange model represents an analytical weakness. Lange does not seem to realize that the convergence properties of the auctioneer's routine are heavily dependent on the *a priori* character of this procedure. Therefore his model does not take up the main advantage of planning: that attempts are made on paper with tickets and do not involve the implementations of inconsistent decisions. On the other hand, Lange's model also does not take into account a cost of planning that exists even under his model of decentralized planning: unlike the mythical Walrasian auctioneer, planning offices and procedures are not free and involve costly administration. However, his insight that the costs of planning can be decreased by decentralizing some decisions to some peripheral units (i.e., firms) have been very fruitful, and other models of decentralized planning have been elaborated in the postwar period. Such models are true planning models, since they assume that an information exchange between the planning office and the firms takes place before the plan is implemented.

The starting point of these models has been a more precise restatement of the Walrasian auctioneer–planner economy put forward by Arrow and Hurwicz (1960).[2] In this model, the planning offices send price vectors to the firms, which maximize their profits, and to a collective consumer, which maximizes the difference between social welfare and costs at those prices. The quantities that solve these maximization problems are sent back to the planning office, which increases (decreases) the price of each commodity for which an excess demand (supply) exists. The procedure is repeated several times until the equilibrium prices are achieved and all the excess demands and supplies are eliminated. Only at this point is the plan considered to be completed and is then implemented.

The Arrow–Hurwicz planning procedure is formalized using a system of differential equations and is therefore assumed to be performed continuously over time. By contrast, price revisions are made by finite steps, at discrete times. The convergence properties of price adjustment working at discrete times have been examined by Uzawa (1958), and they turn out to be weaker, as the planning procedure will converge not to the equilibrium prices but to a price vector whose distance from the equilibrium prices depends on the size of the parameter that indicates the rate of adjustment of prices for given values of excess demands. This creates an unsoluble dilemma for the planning office: what is to be the size of this parameter? While values that are too small will allow prices to converge very near to the equilibrium price vector, many costly iterations are needed for this to occur; on the other hand, a value of the parameter that is too large will imply the contrary.

Moreover, this problem is not the only one arising from the Arrow–Hurwicz–Uzawa model. Malinvaud (1967) has pointed out that this procedure does not satisfy the feasibility and monotonicity properties. In other words, some steps of the planning procedure can imply that no solution is feasible at that step, and the solution of each step is not necessarily superior to (i.e., is not necessarily associated with a higher value of the social welfare than) the solution of the preceding step. These characteristics of the auctioneer–planner model are particularly negative, since in real planning it is possible to carry out only a few iterations. As Kornai (1973) points out, the time that can be employed in formulating the plan is limited. The planning procedure 'cannot begin very early because then there are not yet statistical data close to the action period of the plan. It cannot end too late either, because we would reach into the action period, into the time of executing the plan' (p. 529). The fact that it is possible to carry out only a limited number of interactions makes the feasibility and monotonicity properties of a planning procedure very important, as they assure that, even if we have not achieved the optimum plan, we have not, on the other hand, wasted time.

Other negative aspects of the auctioneer–planner model lie in the rather restrictive assumptions about the economic environment that are necessary to assure convergence of the planning procedure. In particular, the economic environment must be characterized by the absence of constant and increasing returns to scale. (On this point, see also Heal, 1973, p. 107).

The limitations of the auctioneer–planner model have led some economists to formulate alternative planning procedures in which the information flows and/or the calculations performed by the planning bureau are altered in such a way as to obtain more satisfactory characteristics of the planning procedure. Malinvaud (1967) has proposed a planning procedure in which the planning office, instead of changing prices according to excess demand, adopts a more complicated computation rule by which it can acquire an increasing knowledge of the possibilities of substitution that may exist in the productive sphere (see also Heal, 1973). At each stage, the planning bureau sends a price vector to the firms and receives back the net demand vectors that maximize the profits at these prices. At each stages the planning office is supposed to know not only s points in the production possibilities of each firm, but also all the convex linear combinations of the s known points. In this way, the planning office is able to know a larger and larger subset of the set of production possibilities.

Of course, if prices were sent at random, this procedure would only describe a particular way of transmitting all the information concerning the technology of the firms, and Malinvaud's procedure could hardly overcome Hayek's objection that planning is a costly procedure which involves the centralization of information by a single agent. But Malinvaud has shown that it is possible for the planning office to achieve an optimum plan relatively speedily even when it knows only a small proportion of the sets of production possibilities. In order to achieve this result, the planning office at each stage sends the shadow prices associated with the solution of a planning problem. This planning problem is formulated by the planning office on the basis of the knowledge of the firm's production sets which the planning office has at that stage. Unlike Uzawa's auctioneer–planner model, the Malinvaud procedure has the advantage of converging exactly to an optimum. Another advantage lies in the fact that, with a few simple changes, this procedure can be adopted to work under constant returns to scale. Furthermore, it can be shown to satisfy the feasibility, monotonicity and convergence properties (see Malinvaud, 1967).

Another departure from the auctioneer–planner model can be found in a model elaborated by Kornai and Liptak (1965; see also Heal, 1973). A characteristic of this model is that the traditional information flows between the planning office and the firms are inverted. The messages of the planning office to the firms are allocations of inputs to firms; then, in order to gauge the correctness of its allocation, the planning office asks the firms to determine the shadow prices of the central allocations (i.e., the implicit value of each allocation to the firm concerned). At each stage, having received the shadow prices calculated by firms, the planning office tries to adjust the allocations in such a way as to equalize the shadow prices of any input in every sector. For example, if the electricity power quota has a higher shadow price in one firm in comparison with other firms, the planning office will increase the supply of electricity to this firm.

A problem with this model however, is to determine by how much such a quota must be increased. Certainly, if the planning office gives all the electricity power to the firm where it has the highest shadow price, it is very unlikely that we will come closer to the optimum plan. This trouble seems to resemble very closely that of the Uzawa procedure. In fact, it can be shown that in the case of this model, also, the adjustment process converges to within some region of an optimum, the size of this region declining as the step size declines (see Heal, 1973, p. 185). Moreover, only for small steps can the procedure be shown to be monotonic. These characteristics make the Kornai–Liptak procedure inferior to the Malinvaud procedure. On the other hand, an advantage of the Kornai–Liptak procedure is that no restriction has to be made about the characteristics of the technology of the firms, and that the planning office performs a calculation simpler than that of Malinvaud's procedure.

In conclusion, therefore, it seems impossible to state at this level of the analysis whether it is better to decentralize some decisions to the firms in the traditional way rather than by inverting the information flows and having the planning office send quantitative targets instead of prices to the firms. Each of the two methods shows some advantages and some disadvantages. Moreover, as it has been pointed out by Malinvaud, actual planning procedures seem to use both.[3] We are not going to examine this problem; the literature considered above can already be used to illustrate the points that are relevant for the present work. These points can be summarized as follows.

(1) As Hayek pointed out, the costs of central planning in collecting and processing information (and other costs which could also be mentioned) can be so high as to make a planned economy unfeasible.

(2) The costs of planning can be decreased, however, by decentralizing some decisions to the firms. Walras's 'ticket economy' already provided an indication of how this could be done. Although Lange's socialist economy did not completely exploit Walras's suggestion, it certainly inclined in this direction. Not only has the planning literature reinterpreted the Walrasian economy as a planned economy, but it has also shown how the performance properties of the 'ticket economy' can be strengthened when this interpretation is explicitly made – that is, either by altering the information flows between the planning office and the agents (Kornai–Liptak), or by altering the computation rules of the planning office (Malinvaud).

(3) The observation that planning is a costly activity involves decisions concerning the organization of production that should be taken by the managers of the firms. In particular, the managers are usually assumed to take these decisions according to a profit-maximizing rule. The existence of profit-maximizing managers can therefore be a characteristic of a planned society. On the other hand, we saw in the preceding chapter that profit maximization is consistent with the maximization of social welfare only if a price exists for each one of the tasks performed by the workers. By contrast, manpower is treated in this model as a homogeneous resource (since the 'leisure device' is adopted). If the preferences of the workers are to be taken into account, an (accounting) price should be computed for each one of the different tasks. But this is likely to increase the costs of the planning procedure by increasing the dimension of the messages that have to be exchanged at each stage. Although it is inconsistent with the aim of taking into account the preferences of the workers, the internal allocation of a profit-maximizing manager (and therefore his authority) could be defended on the ground that it reduces the costs of coordinating economic activity.

2   Centralizing decisions in the firms

We have seen how the literature examined in the previous sections has led to the idea that some units such as firms should exist, and that some decisions should be decentralized to them because the use of planning is costly. R. Coase (1953) can be considered the founder of a converging stream of the literature, which has explained the existence of the firm from the astute observation that the use of the market is also costly.

Let us return to the Hayek objection to planning. Hayek maintained that planning was either impossible or wasteful because of the difficulties involved in collecting and processing information about consumer tastes and firms' technology. Market prices, on the other hand, were described as efficient transmitters of information. The agents of the market economy needed only to know market prices to coordinate their decisions. An efficient coordination of individual's actions could be achieved completely through the price system.

A striking implication of Hayek's statement is that each subunit of the economy should not contain more than one member, and hence that it is useless for either a central planner or even the manager of a smaller organization to coordinate production. Market prices should be the only coordinating mechanism.

In his article, 'The Nature of the Firm', Coase observed that Hayek's position was in clear conflict with the existence of firms in the economy. Coase regarded the firm not only as a possible agent of the market economy, but also as an institution within which production decisions are coordinated in a way that differs from the operation of the market mechanism.

> Outside the firm, price movements direct production which is coordinated through a series of exchange transactions on the market. Within a firm, these market transactions are eliminated and in place of the complicated market structure with exchange transactions is substituted and the entrepreneur coordinator, who directs production. (Coase, 1953, p. 333)

According to Coase, market prices coordinate production only outside the firm. By contrast, within the firm, production factors are allocated according to a very different coordination mechanism. In a firm, If a workman moves from department Y to department X, he does not go because of a change in relative prices but because he is ordered to do so.' Within the firm, the horizontal relationship between buyer and seller is replaced by the hierarchical relationship between employer and employee, or the 'master-servant relationship'. Quite rightly, Coase rejects the argument that 'the reason for the existence of the firm is to be found in the division of labour.' Also, the price mechanism constitutes a way of organizing the division of labour. Moreoever, what 'has to be explained is why one integrating force (the entrepreneur) should be substituted for another integrating force (the price mechanism)' (1953, pp. 333, 344).

According to Coase, therefore, market exchanges and the firm are two alternative mechanisms through which the same processes can be coordinated. Within the firm, planning replaces the coordinating role of the market price movements. The fact that planning (within the firm) and market exchange co-exist within any so-called market economy makes Coase formulate the following objection to those who, like Hayek, had maintained that planning was a costly or even unfeasible surrogate for the market system:

> Those who object to economic planning on the grounds that the problem is solved by price movements can be answered by pointing out that there is planning within our economic system which is quite different from ... individual planning ... and which is akin to what is normally called economic planning. (Coase, 1953, p. 333)

Coase's approach to the problem may appear quite unnecessary to anyone who is aware of Marx's contribution in this field. As we have seen, Marx had clearly pointed out that the firm and the market were two alternative ways of coordinating production, and had conceived socialist planning as an extension of firm-type coordination to the whole economy. Moreover, Denis Robertson had already pointed out, in his brilliant Cambridge Economic Handbook, *The Control of Industry* (1928), that the coordinating mechanism of firms was quite different from that operating under the market system. He aptly described firms as 'islands of conscious power in an ocean of unconscious co-operation' which looked 'like lumps of butter coagulating in a pail of butter-milk' (p. 85). Yet, these achievements had had a very limited impact on the development of orthodox economic analysis and had been completely ignored in the course of the debate about socialism (a notable exception being Robertson, 1928, itself). Thus, Coase's suggestion that 'the use of the word "firm" in economics may be different from the use of the term "plain man"' (p. 331) constituted by itself an important contribution to the debate, even if this observation could hardly be considered an original one.

Now, if the firm and the market constitute two different forms of coordination, one based on planning and the other on price movements, how can we explain that, even in our system, decisions are not entirely coordinated by price movements, and planning activity exists? Coase's answer is based on the fact that, if it is true that planning activity is costly (as Hayek maintains), the use of the market mechanism is also costly (as Hayek fails to emphasize). He explains the existence of the firm, therefore, by pointing out the costs that would otherwise be incurred if market transactions were used for coordinating production.[4] 'The most obvious cost of "organizing" production through the price mechanism is that of discovering what the relevant prices are. This cost may be reduced but it will not be eliminated by the emergence of specialists who will sell this information' (p. 336). The cost of negotiating a contract should also be considered; again, this can be reduced but not eliminated by the emergence of specialists. But these costs can be greatly reduced by the existence of firms:

> A factor of production (or the owner thereof) does not have to make a series of contracts with the factors with whom he is cooperating within the firm, as would be necessary, of course, if this cooperation were as a direct result of the workings of the price mechanism. For this series of contracts is substituted one ... whereby the factor for a certain remuneration (which may be fixed or fluctuating) agrees to obey the directions of an entrepreneur *within certain limits*. (Coase, 1953, pp. 336–7)

The usefulness of the employment relationship, or the 'master–servant' relationship, is explained by Coase within this framework. Quoting Batt's (1933) book, *The Law of Master and Servant*, Coase characterizes this relationship as a particular, but also the most important, case of the substitution of market coordination for firm-type coordination. In the employment relationship, the master makes a single contract with each servant for the many tasks that the servant may perform for him. Then, within the limits set by the employment contract, the master acquires

> the right to control the servant's work, either personally or through another servant or agent. It is this right of control or interference, of being entitled to tell the servant when to work (within the hours of service) and when not to work, and what work to do and how to do it (within the terms of such service), which is the dominant characteristic in this relation and marks off the servant from an independent contractor, or from one employed merely to give to his employer the fruits of his labour. (Batt, 1933, p. 6)

In other words, using the terminology of the preceding chapter, the employment contract is characterized by the fact that the employer acquires the right to deploy the employee among alternative tasks. And this right, which characterizes the master-servant or the employer–employee relationship and the nature of the firm itself, is justified by Coase on the ground that it reduces the costs of organizing economic activity by substituting a single market transaction for many (costly) transactions.

On the other hand, Coase is also aware of the fact that firm-type coordination is costly. And these latter costs explain why all production is not carried on by one big firm. He believes that after a certain point it becomes impossible for a single entrepreneur to coordinate production, and that the costs of organizing additional transactions within the firm may increase with the size of the firm. This circumstance explains why market-type and firm-type coordination can co-exist within the same economic system.[5]

The peculiar nature of the employment contract which characterizes the firm has also been the object of the work of H. Simon. Although Simon does not seem to be aware of Coase's contribution, which is never quoted in his two papers relating to this problem,[6] he shares with Coase a very similar definition of the employment contract, which Simon contrasts with the sales contract. The employment contract, he says, means that, in exchange for a given wage, the employee (or 'worker') agrees to accept the authority of the employer and the employer is allowed to decide which particular actions the worker will perform. Of course, the employer cannot choose any kind of action to be performed by the worker; his authority is restricted to a certain subset of the possible actions, which Simon calls the 'area of acceptance' of the worker (Simon, 1957, p. 184). The employment contract 'differs fundamentally from a sales contract – the kind of contract that is assumed in ordinary formulations of price theory. In the sales contract, each party promises a specific consideration in return for the consideration promised by the other' (p. 184). In other words, in the sales contract the buyer (in our case the boss) promises the seller (in our case the worker) to pay a certain sum of money against a specified quantity of a completely specified commodity. No exercise of authority is therefore exercised by the buyer at a later date in the sales contract, since the contract completely specifies the obligations of each of the parties. Simon observes that 'certain services are obtained by buyers in our society sometimes by a sales contract, sometimes by an employment contract', and considers the circumstances likely to favour one or the other kind of contract. As he himself points out, his whole argument centres on the fact that 'the employment relationships is "a rational" adjustment to ignorance about the future' (p. 198). The buyer of manpower does not know in advance which particular task to be performed by the worker in the future will maximize his profits, and he cannot specify, without risk of losses, which task the worker has to perform. A sales contract would involve a specification of the tasks that the buyer of manpower wants the worker to perform – a specification that may well be impossible or at least risky under conditions of uncertainty about future events. When these conditions prevail, the sales contract is likely to be replaced by an employment contract. In such a case, using Coase's terminology, we could say that the firm replaces market transactions in the coordination of some economic decisions.

It could be objected that sales contracts would not necessarily imply a decision in advance on which particular set of tasks the workers will perform if it is possible to sign conditional contracts (or contracts in contigent commodities). The existence of uncertainty does imply that we do not know which state of the world we are going to deal with (and therefore which particular amounts of tasks and goods will maximize profits); however, in such circumstances we could say that each unit contract is either for the delivery of a one unit good or for performing a certain task if a specified state of the world has occurred. When this device is accepted, the existence of uncertainty implies only an increase in the number of contracts and commodities traded in the market. No guess at the particular state of the world (and therefore of the amounts of tasks and goods that will maximize profits) is necessary, therefore, if it is possible to trade in contingent commodities. But these additional contracts would imply an increase of the market transaction costs, pointed out by Coase, which the firm (and the employment contract) is intended to save. Moreover, it is possible to see how costly or even impracticable this solution can be by introducing the principle of bounded rationality put forward by Simon himself.

'The capacity of the human mind', he points out, 'for formulating and solving complex problems is very small compared with the size of the problems whose solution is required for objectively rational behaviour in the real world or even for a reasonable approximation to such objective rationality' (p. 198). As Williamson has observed, it is the coupling of bounded rationality and uncertainty that can be the cause of a shift from market coordination to internal organization. The employment contract has the advantage of economizing on bounded rationality since it implies that it is not necessary to know the consequences of each state of the world – a knowledge necessary for writing contracts in contingent commodities which may even exceed the capacity of the human mind. The employment contract allows the employer to decide the task that the employee has to perform in a certain state of the world only when this stage occurs, so that it is not necessary to know in advance all the possible states of the world.

Another circumstance, according to O. E. Williamson (1975), that can determine a shift from market relations to hierarchical organizations as firms is the coupling of a small number of relations and opportunism. 'Opportunism extends the conventional assumption that economic agents are guided by considerations of self-interest to make allowance for strategic behaviour. This involves self-interest seeking with guile and has profound implications for choosing between alternative relationships' (Williamson, 1975, p. 26). If many competitors exist in the market, this will make opportunistic inclinations largely ineffectual. Individuals or organizations who have tried to secure gains by opportunistic behaviour are likely are likely not to have their contracts renewed. 'When, however, opportunism is joined by a small-numbers condition, the trading situation is greatly transformed' (p. 27). Opportunistic behaviour is not anymore made ineffectual by competition, and the bargaining costs are likely to increase since each party is interested in seeking terms most favourable to her, which encourages opportunistic representation and haggling. Small numbers either can exist *ex ante*, when a contract is first signed, or can appear *ex post*, at the contract renewal. 'If parity among supplies is upset by first-mover advantages, so that winners of original bids subsequently enjoy non-trivial cost-advantages over non-winners, the sales relationship that eventually obtains is effectively of the small-numbers variety' (p. 28).

The fact that a small-numbers relation can either exist *ex ante* or emerge *ex post*, when the contract has been implemented, can make it convenient to shift from a sales relationship (or a market relationship) to an employment contract (or a form of hierarchical control). In fact, according to Williamson, internal coordination has some advantages over market-type coordination in cases where opportunism and small-numbers conditions prevail. The members of the same organization are more likely to share the feeling that they are all in the same boat, and this can reduce opportunistic behaviour. Moreover, internal organization can be more effectively audited. This role can be performed by an auditor within a firm; and, an internal auditor has the advantage over an external one of having more information and access about the performance of members of the organization. Consequently, opportunistic behaviour can be more easily monitored within an organization. Finally, within an organization, litigations among members can be solved more easily than litigations that would otherwise occur among automonous contractors. Within an organization an internal member whose commitment to the goals of the organization and whose authority is accepted by both parties can solve these disputes. By contrast, when a dispute arises between automonous contractors, arbitration costs are likely to be higher, since it is more difficult to find an individual whose authority will be accepted by both sides.

These advantages in preventing and solving disputes which internal organizations have in comparison with the market are also clearly evident in situations involving both uncertainty and opportunism. We have seen that the market could efficiently deal with situations of uncertainty if it were possible to exchange commodities contingent upon all the possible states of the world, and that this solution cannot be adopted for solving (at least completely) the problem of uncertainty because of transaction costs and bounded rationality. There is, however, an additional difficulty with contracts contingent upon a particular state of the world: the two parties who have agreed to sign the contract can at a later date disagree about the particular state of the world with which they are dealing – a circumstance that is likely to arise if they behave opportunistically. The existence of these disputes can create a situation in which market transaction costs are very high; and a shift to internal organization may be convenient, given the advantages it possesses in preventing and solving litigations. In particular, we can see how the employment contract can do better than a sales contract in this situation. The former does not specify which amount of each particular task the employee will have to perform in a particular state of the world; such a choice is left (within certain limits or within a certain area of acceptance) to the employer. Disputes concerning the nature of the state of the world that is faced by the agents are therefore less likely to occur.

In conclusion, the literature examined above has concentrated on the fact that market and firm constitute two alternative allocation mechanisms and that the existence of the firm has therefore to be justified and explained by referring to its advantages over the market mechanism. This insight is not new, since it was very clearly pointed out by Marx (an author that this literature seems to ignore), although some of the arguments by which the existence of the firm is justified are different from those employed by him (see chapter 3, section 2.2). There is, however, one particular argument employed by Marx, which is not recalled in this literature and may be worth repeating: namely, that the firm is a planned island in the market economy and as such enjoys the advantages of *ex ante* coordination. Such an argument has been ignored by the literature, which has concentrated mainly on the equilibrium situation. Once the equilibrium has been achieved, the nature of the adjustment mechanism (i.e., *ex ante* or *ex post*) becomes irrelevant. But it *can* be relevant for understanding why firms exist, and why some 'degree' of planning can be necessary in the economy.

3 Two converging literatures

I will conclude this chapter by pointing out the symmetry between the two streams of the literature that have been examined in the preceding sections. As an ideal starting point of both streams, we can consider Hayek's observation that planning involves costly administration owing to the fact that it requires the collection and processing of a vast amount of information – a waste avoided in the market system, where market prices provide the information that is necessary in order for agents to take decisions. From Hayek's observation that planning is a costly activity, the planning literature has derived the incentive to work out planning procedures that can reduce the costs of economic planning by decentralizing some decisions to firms (usually by the use of accounting prices). By contrast, the literature examined in section 2 has observed that Hayek's statement seems to ignore the fact that there are some costs also of using the market mechanism. These costs can be reduced by centralizing some decisions to non-market organizations such as firms.

In both streams of the literature, the firm emerges, either because of the costs of planning or because of the costs of using the market price mechanism, as an indispensable unit for taking economic decisions. The problem that we are going to discuss in the next chapter is how decisions should be taken within this unit if the preferences of the workers are to be taken into account.

Notes

1 The page numbers will refer to Farrel (1973).
2 A lucid exposition of the model is also contained in Heal (1973).
3 'It would therefore be desirable', Malinvaud (1967, p. 207) has pointed out, 'to search for procedures in which the prospective indices combine production targets with indicative prices for the different commodities. In this way, we would draw nearer to the methods used in practice, and would be able to deduce more directly usable conclusions from our theoretical studies.'
4 Also, this kind of explanation was not new, even if Coase has the merit of having given to it the emphasis that it deserves. Marshall had very well understood its importance as it results from the following passage: 'But a great point of marketing consists of bargaining or manoeuvering to get others to buy at a high price and sell at a low price, to obtain special concessions or to force a trade by offering them. This, from the social point of view, is almost pure waste; it is that part of trade as to which Aristotele's dictum is most nearly true, that no one can gain except at the loss of another. It has a great attraction for some minds that are not merely mean, but nevertheless is the only part of honest trade competition that is entirely devoid of any enabling or elevating feature. A claim is made on behalf of large firms and large combinations that their growth tends to diminish the waste, and in the whole perhaps it does' (Marshall, 1890, pp. 109-10).
5 According to Coase, firms will expand only up to the point where 'the costs of organizing within the firm will be equal either to the costs of organizing in another firm or to the costs involved in leaving the transaction to be "organized" by the price mechanism' (1953, p. 350).
6 See H. A. Simon, 'A Comparison of Organization Theories', *Review of Economic Studies*, vol. 29, and 'A Formal Theory of the Employment Relation', *Econometrica*, vol. 19; both republished in Simon (1957).

9

Profit maximization v. democracy at the workplace (or, some means are also ends)

1 A normative dilemma

In chapter 7 we saw that, when the leisure device is not adopted and the preferences of the workers for the allocation of their work are taken into account, the internal allocation of a profit-maximizing manager is in general inconsistent with the allocation of work that maximizes social welfare. We therefore concluded that, when these preferences *are* taken into account, the optimization problem that society faces can be solved in two ways: (a) by a complete set of market prices (one for each task being performed) or (2) by an omniscient central planner – both solutions being characterized by the absence of firms' internal allocation. However, we then saw that these solutions ignore both the costs of using the market and the planning mechanisms which we examined in chapter 8.

A market price for each task would involve a dramatic increase in market transactions and, presumably, in market transaction costs, in comparison with the situation in which the internal allocation is performed by a profit-maximizing manager and a single transaction is held for labour-power independently of the tasks to be performed in production. When the relative costs of market transactions and the internal allocation of a profit-maximizing manager are taken into account, it is no longer true that the allocation effected using only market transactions is (necessarily) superior to the internal allocation of a profit-maximizing manager. The cost of firm-type coordination may be so much lower than the cost of market transactions that this offsets the welfare loss due to the inconsistency of the internal allocation of work effected by a profit-maximizing manager with the allocation maximizing social welfare. The greater costs of market transactions may well nullify the welfare gain due to the fact that, unlike profit-maximizing managers, the market takes into account workers' preferences.

With regard to centralized planning, taking into account the preferences of workers for the work they do would certainly increase the costs of the planning procedure because it would mean that more data have to be collected and processed by the planning office.

The case of decentralized planning recalls very closely the case of the market. With decentralized planning, accounting prices are used in the information exchanges between the planning board and the peripheral units. These exchanges of information cannot be considered to be free since they cost time and other scarce resources. Clearly, the cost involved will depend on the number of messages (prices and quantities) to be transmitted. If the preferences of workers have to be taken into account, a message will have to be exchanged and an accounting price computed for each task, since the internal allocation of labour can no longer be left to the profit-maximizing (socialist) managers. Such an increase in the number of messages to be exchanged will determine an increase in the costs of the decentralized planning procedure, the size of which could even offset the welfare benefits obtained by taking into account the workers' preferences.

There seems, therefore, to be an unfortunate trade-off between two desirable goals. On the one hand, we would wish to take into account the preferences of workers. This implies an increase in the number of transactions, in the case of the market system, and in the number of variables to be computed, in a decentralized planned economy. On the other hand, we would wish to reduce the costs of coordinating economic activity. But this may well imply that the number of market transactions, or the number of prices to be computed in the case of a decentralized planning system, should be decreased by letting a profit-maximizing manager allocate manpower within its firm.

In the next section we will consider a way out of this dilemma with particular reference to a market economy (assumed to be in equilibrium). Then, given the analogy outlined above, the solution arrived at for the market economy will be extended to the case of a decentralized planned economy.

2 *Internalizing workers' preferences*

2.1 *The case of a market economy*

In terms of the model used in chapter 7, the dilemma outlined in the preceding section can be restated in the following way. At the one extreme we have the situation that is described in proposition 5.1, of that chapter, where market transaction costs are very low since only n market transactions are necessary in order for manpower to be allocated in the economy. We know, however, that this allocation maximizes social welfare only in the case where we assume that members of society have no preferences for different uses for manpower in production, and this is in general inconsistent with the social welfare maximum condition ((5.3') in chapter 7). At the other extreme, we have the situation described in proposition 5.2 of chapter 7. In this case, the opposite circumstance applies. While the optimum social welfare conditions are satisfied under the more general and realistic assumption that the uses of manpower affect social utility, market transaction costs are high. The allocation of manpower is completely contracted in the market, and $n \times T$ market transactions are therefore required. While in the first case only an overall price of manpower is required in order for manpower to be allocated among the different firms, in the latter case a price should exist for each different task.

Of course, our dilemma does not imply such extreme choices as either not taking into account the preferences of the workers for their work or not considering the remarkable increase in transaction costs that this consideration involves; some intermediate solutions are possible. There is, however, an unfortunate trade-off between satisfying the social welfare optimum condition ((5.3') in chapter 7) and reducing market transaction costs by internalizing some transactions within the profit-maximizing firm.

Is there a way out of this dilemma? Is is possible to create economic institutions such that the social welfare optimum conditions can be satisfied without such a dramatic increase of transaction costs? In other words, is it possible to adopt a form of organization of the economy that has only the good qualities of the two extreme cases described above?

Let us try to make these questions more precise. They are tantamount to asking whether there exists an institutional framework such that the two following conditions are satisfied.

Condition 2.1   The standard welfare condition (i.e., condition (5.3′) in chapter 7) is satisfied, as in the case in which the allocation of a human resource is completely realized using market transactions.

Condition 2.2   The number of transactions is the same as when the firm's internal allocation by profit-maximizing managers is allowed – i.e., the number of transactions is n and not $n \times T$.

For this purpose, we will consider the following institutional framework. As in section 5 of chapter 7, we assume that a distributor exists in the economy, which maximizes the difference between the utility and the costs of the products; i.e.,

$$U_0(y_0, y) - \sum_{i=1}^{n} \lambda_i y_i - \lambda_R y_0. \qquad (2.1)$$

However, unlike the case examined in chapter 7, we assume that n workers' cooperatives exist in the economy. Each one of them is assumed to maximize

$$U_i(x_i) + \lambda_i y_i - \lambda_R \sum_j x_{ij} \quad i = 1, \ldots, n \qquad (2.2)$$

where x_i is the vector of the T tasks that are performed in the ith cooperative. The cooperative's objective function is different from the objective function of a profit-maximizing firm since it also takes into account the utility or disutility that is derived from performing the different tasks. Profit maximization is therefore a particular case of maximizing the cooperative objective function that arises when the latter circumstance is not taken into account.

We will assume that the trade-offs between tasks in each cooperative are independent of the trade-offs between different consumption goods and between consumption goods and leisure. While an interdependence between these trade-offs could easily be considered by increasing the number of arguments of the function that each cooperative and the distributor maximize, it seems realistic to assume that 'a certain degree' of separability of the welfare function exists. We will therefore make the following assumption.

Assumption 2.1

$$U(y_0, y, x_1, \ldots, x_n) = U_0(y_0, y) + U_1(x_1)$$
$$+ \ldots + U_i(x_i) + \ldots + U_n(x_n).$$

We can now consider the following two propositions.

Proposition 2.1   Under A2.1, A5.1, A2.3 and A2.4(b) of chapter 7 and A2.1 above, it is possible to decentralize a social optimum to a distributor who maximizes (2.1) and to n workers' cooperatives who maximize (2.2), provided there exists a set of shadow prices $\lambda_0, \lambda_1, \ldots, \lambda_n, \lambda_R$, one for each output and one for manpower.

Proof   Maximizing (2.1) and (2.2) gives us the following first-order necessary conditions:

$$U_{0_{y_i}} \leqslant \lambda_i \tag{2.3}$$

$$U_{0_{y_0}} \leqslant \lambda_R \tag{2.4}$$

$$U_{i_{x_{ij}}} + \lambda_i f^i_{x_{ij}} \leqslant \lambda_R \tag{2.5}$$

which, because of A2.1 above, are equivalent to conditions (5.1')–(5.3') and (5.5') of chapter 7.

Proposition 2.2   Under A2.1, A5.1, A2.3 and A2.4(b) of chapter 7 and A2.1 above, the institutional framework, which is defined by the distributor who maximizes (2.1) and the n workers' cooperatives that maximize (2.2), satisfies conditions (2.1) and (2.2) above.

Proof   This follows immediately from proposition 2.1 above.

Thus, the replacement of n profit-maximizing firms by n workers' cooperatives implies that the social welfare optimum conditions can be satisfied by an institutional framework, which defines these conditions, without increasing the number of market transactions. This occurs because the internal allocation of manpower within the workers' cooperative is not inconsistent with the allocation that is required by the social optimum conditions.

A cooperative i allocates a certain amount of manpower maximizing

$$U_i(x_i) + \lambda_i y_i$$

$$\text{subject to } \sum_j x_{ij} \leqslant \bar{L}_i$$

which implies that condition (5.7) of chapter 7, which is necessary for a social optimum, is satisfied.

We can observe, finally, that de-skilling jobs and technological efficiency do not necessarily characterize the choices of a cooperative, while they do necessarily characterize the choices of a profit-maximizing manager who allocates a certain endowment of labour-power within his firm. This difference arises from the fact that the objective function of the cooperative is to consider not only the output being produced but also the (dis)utility that is derived by the time spent at work. De-skilling jobs and technological efficiency, while increasing the revenue ($\lambda_i y_i$) of the cooperative, might imply an allocation that is characterized by a strong increase in disutility of the tasks being performed. In this case, the choice of the profit-maximizing manager and that of the cooperative will necessarily diverge.

2.2   The case of planning

A similar conclusion can be reached if we interpret the prices of the model not as market equilibrium prices but as accounting prices, which have been calculated by a central planner using, for instance, an auctioneer–planner model. In this case, when preferences for different tasks are taken into account, the number of messages (accounting prices) that the planning office needs to issue must increase from 1 to ($n \times T$) prices if the socialist firms are to maximize profits. Such a large number of messages to be issues at any stage of the planning procedure is extremely likely to increase the costs of (decentralized) planning in the same way as an increase in the number of market transactions is likely to increase the costs of using the market mechanism. In the case of planning, the replacement of n profit-maximizing firms by n workers' cooperatives reduces the number of accounting prices from ($n \times T$) to 1, thus reducing the costs of using the decentralized planning mechanism. Fewer messages have to be sent to the cooperatives because they can take more decisions (without violating the optimality conditions). Also, the cooperatives take the preferences of workers into account in their internal allocations – an aspect of the problem ignored by a profit-maximizing manager.

3   Conclusion

We can now try to summarize the argument by considering how the preferences of workers for their own work can be taken into account under alternative assumptions about the costs of planned and market systems.

(1) If we assume that the costs of using market mechanisms are very low, then individuals' actions can be coordinated entirely using market prices. In this case, the preferences of workers for different uses of their work can be taken into account simply by increasing the number of market transactions and market prices. If the workers are assumed to have no preferences as between the different tasks, a price will exist only for each skill used in production. By contrast, if the workers do have preferences for different tasks, a price will have to exist for each task (see chapter 7, section 5).

We can describe this increase in the number of market prices by saying that taking workers' preferences into account implies a change from a market price vector p_m to a price vector P_m, where the number of the components of P_m is greater than the number of components of p_m. We can visualize this effect of workers' preferences as follows:

$$p_m \rightarrow P_m.$$

(2) Let us now assume that market transactions are fairly costly, and that, following Coase's argument (chapter 8, section 3), the market transactions have been internalized within the firms. Society is therefore partially coordinated by the market price system and partially coordinated by those 'planned islands' that are the firms. This mixed type of coordination can be briefly indicated by (p_m, f) where f stands for firms. In this case, when members of society are indifferent to different uses of their manpower in production, the allocation of work within the firm can be decided by profit-maximizing managers on the basis of skill prices only. However, when individuals do have preferences for different tasks, then the internal allocation of a profit-maximizing manager is inconsistent with the maximization of social welfare.

If we want to take workers' preferences into account, we can consider going back to the solution outlined under (1) and coordinating the economy by means of market transactions alone. But we are now assuming that non-market organizations such as firms exist in the economy precisely because of the costs of using the market system. In these circumstances, increasing the number of market transactions and market prices and getting rid of firm-internal allocation processes can be a costly and even impracticable solution. An alternative solution is to substitute workers' coopera-tives (i.e., organizations that internalize the utility function of the workers for their work – see section 2.1 above) for the profit-maximizing firms. In this case, market prices and cooperatives (p_m, c) are used to coordinate economic activity instead of market prices and firms (p_m, f). We can visualize the consequence of taking workers preferences into account as follows:

$$(p_m, f) \rightarrow (p_m, c).$$

(3) Let us now assume that the market transactions are even more costly than in case (2). This can imply that decentralized planning (or a rather extreme centralization of transactions on the lines advocated by Walras – see chapter 6, section 3) can be a better way of coordinating the firms' and the individuals' decisions. Since we also assume that planning is a costly activity (even if less costly than adjustment based on market price movements), some decisions will have to be decentralized to the firms. In particular, we may think that in these circumstances a planning office would decentralize some decisions to the firms by using accounting prices, calculated by a planning office using a decentralized planning procedure, and firms (p_a, f) would then coordinate the economy. If the workers have no preferences among the tasks to be performed, then firms' managers can allocate manpower within the firm on the basis of the accounting prices of skills according to a profit-maximizing rule. On the other hand, if the workers do have preferences for the tasks to be performed, then, again, the internal allocation of a profit-maximizing manager is incompatible with the maximization of social welfare. As in the preceding case, we could try to solve the problem by increasing the number of accounting prices (rather than market prices). In other words, the planning office, theoretically, could also calculate all task prices. However, this solution also is likely to be either too costly or quite impracticable. The firm, as a decisional sub-unit within which certain decisions are taken, has been introduced in the literature to decrease the costs of economic planning (see chapter 8, section 2). An increase of the number of prices to be computed by the planning office is likely to be very costly. An alternative solution can be, again, to substitute workers' cooperatives for the profit-maximizing firms and leave the number of accounting prices calculated by the planning office unchanged. As a consequence of this change, we would have accounting prices and cooperatives (p_a, c) instead of accounting prices and firms

(p_a, f) coordinating the economy. We can visualize this way of taking workers' preferences into account as follows:

$$(p_a, f) \rightarrow (p_a, c).$$

(4) If we assume that the cost of using the planning mechanism is very low, then society can be entirely coordinated by central planning. If the workers have no preferences among alternative uses of their manpower, then society should be organized as a single 'big firm' which maximizes the outputs of production in the proportions desired by its members. However, if the workers do care for the allocation of their work, it is necessary to replace this 'big firm' with one 'big cooperative' which takes into account the (dis)utility that the workers derive from the kind of work that they perform as well as the utility derived from the products of labour. Since we are now assuming that the cost of planning is very low, taking into account workers' preferences does not constitute a problem, although it increases the number of unknowns to be determined by the planning office. (This case therefore recalls the first case, where it was assumed that the cost of using market transactions was very low.) Thus, if preferences for work are to be taken into account, society can switch its organization from one single big firm (F) to one big cooperative (C); i.e.,

$$F \rightarrow C.$$

We can now try to collate these four points in 'a table of organizations'. We will assume that, reading from left to right of our table, the opportunity cost of using market transactions (i.e., the forgone benefit of using planning) increases. The far left[1] of the table indicates one extreme situation where the cost of market transactions is very low and the cost of planning very high. The far right of the table indicates the opposite situation. The case in which workers' preferences are not taken into account is indicated

Workers' preferences		Opportunity cost of using market transactions increases		
No	p_m	(f, p_m)	(f, p_a)	F
Yes	P_m	(c, p_m)	(c, p_a)	C

in the first row, whereas the case in which they are taken into account is indicated in the second row. The centralized planning and complete market solutions (i.e., solutions (4) and (1) above, respectively) are chosen in the two extreme cases where the costs of using market transactions and the costs of using planning are very low. The market with 'planned islands', such as firms or cooperatives, and the decentralized planning solutions (solutions (2) and (3), respectively) occupy an intermediate region between these two extremes.

Of course, this simple table cannot pretend to exhaust all the possible ways in which economic activity can be coordinated. Moreover, intermediate solutions between those indicated in the table are not only possible, but constitute the most common cases in modern economies. Market and planning co-exist in many economies; and they do for the very simple reason that the costs of planning and market change in the different sectors of the economy and according to the actions that have to be coordinated. Furthermore, the employment contract can be considered as an intermediate solution between P_m and (f, p_m). This does not usually specify the price of each task to be performed, implying that the employer has the authority to decide which particular task the worker should undertake, but it does usually specify the limits and the conditions of this exercise of authority (see chapter 8, section 3).

Yet the table is in my opinion very useful for understanding why the problem of the extension of democracy to the workplace has not received the attention that it deserves, from either Marxist or orthodox economists. Such an oversight can be partially explained by saying that the literature has concentrated on the two extremes of the table. Hirschman (1970) has argued that, in the ideal world of orthodox theoretical economics, workers can vote with their feet, since they can leave (exit from) the firms whenever they are dissatisfied with management, and move to better conditions. If market transactions were not costly, the 'exit mechanism' would ensure a complete expression of workers' preferences; then it would be possible to exit from each single task and in this way express preferences. In terms of our table, we can say that the ideal world of theoretical economics coincides with the case indicated at the far left. Here, the existence of workers' preferences for their tasks simply involves more market transactions and more prices, and therefore the possibility of more exits. And since the cost of these additional market transactions is assumed to be very low, the problem of expressing the preferences of the workers by means other than the market mechanism does not arise in this framework. In Hirschman's words, the problem of using 'voice' cannot arise because 'exit' is considered as a way in which preferences can be cheaply expressed. In other words, the problem of the extension of democracy to the workplace cannot arise in the framework of orthodox theoretical economics, even where the 'leisure device' is not adopted and the preferences of the workers for their work are taken into account.

At the risk of being rather schematic, we can see the Marxian approach at the other extreme of our table, where the costs of planning are assumed to be very low. We saw that a great advantage of Marx over Smith – and, indeed, over the majority of the later economic theorists – lay in the explicit observation that under capitalism both firms and markets coordinate economic activity (chapter 3, section 1.2). Marx regarded the planned system implemented within the firm as a system far more efficient than the market.

His model of a socialist society was in fact a single-firm society in which a 'chief employer' rationally allocated labour (chapter 3, section 1.3). In terms of our table, Marx proposed that society should switch from (p_m, f) to F. In this first switch, work could be treated as an homogeneous good. As we saw in chapter 3, this assumption did not rely on the fact that the preferences of the workers for their work were not important; indeed Marx is still, in my view, the main source of inspiration for whoever thinks that work cannot be treated like iron or corn or any other non-human factor of production. Instead, we have seen that he believed that the power of the profit-maximizing capitalists had expropriated from the workers their possibility of expressing their preferences for their work. And orthodox economics can challenge this statement only for the case in which profit-maximizing managers do not have the authority to allocate the workers among different tasks independently of market transactions. But this is the case in which neither the employment contract nor the firm itself exists. In Marxian terms, this is not the case of capitalism, which involves the sale of labour-power.

Under capitalism, Marx says, not only did the profit-maximizing behaviour of the capitalists not consider the preferences of the workers, but it also destroyed the possibility for them to express these preferences, by de-skilling jobs and making each job similar to another. In other words, capitalism made labour homogeneous from the point of view of the preferences of the workers, and this was the situation that would confront a socialist at the beginning.

A second switch – to a communist society, where not only would the preferences of the workers have to be taken fully into account, but work would become so pleasant as to be considered an end in itself – was postponed to a later period (chapter 3, sections 2.3 and 3). In terms of our table, this second switch implied a change from a model of a single-firm socialist society (F) to a communist society, which can be conceived as a single cooperative society (C), where all work has become pleasant. Marx seemed to conceive this switch as the natural process of evolution of a socialist society and linked it quite mechanically with the development of the productive forces (chapter 3, section 3). This view depends on the fact that he did not appreciate certain of the costs of economic planning. These costs can be such that a single-firm society may be impracticable or at least very costly. Moreover, they are very likely to rise if the workers' preferences have to be taken into account. But Marx's most dangerous oversight about the costs of economic planning is probably found in his view of the planners them-selves. He did not perceive that the planners, and whoever is in a privileged position of power under a socialist regime, would be very likely to have an interest in *not* recognizing the preferences of the workers and in believing (and making others believe) that human labour could be scientifically and efficiently allocated like any other non-human resource.

We saw in chapter 7 that economic science, with its leisure device and its rules of dictatorship, was well suited to support the planners in this belief. If labour could be scientifically allo-cated in an optimum way within a firm according to technological efficiency, de-skilling and profit-maximization rules, then this would also be true for society as a whole in a single-firm economy.

In the Marxian framework, the switch to a society where workers' preferences are taken into account was therefore con-sidered a costless movement, and one that a socialist society would eventually make. It was, therefore, considered a non-issue, similar to the (opposite) case in which market transactions are assumed to be costless. Referring again to Hirschman's terminology, we can say that, just as in orthodox economics, the assumption that market transactions are free implies that the use of the 'exit' is a costless mechanism for expressing preferences; so in the Marxian approach the undervaluation of the costs of planning makes 'voice' a costless means of expressing society's preferences.

But the concentration of these two main approaches on the two extreme cases of our table only partially explains why the issue of the extension of democracy to the workplace has not attracted the attention of economic theory. After all, the decentralized planning literature and the literature about the nature of the firm have involved a considerable switch from the extremes to the centre of our table (from F to (f, p_a) and from p_m to (f, p_m), respectively). However, the explicit recognition that within the firm the market mechanism is (at least partially) superseded has not been taken to mean, for the literature about the nature of the firm, that an alternative to the market should be found which would allow workers to express their preferences about the organization of production. In the same way, the decentralized planning literature has advocated the decentralization of decisions to profit-maximizing managers but not to organizations that express the preferences of the workers (see chapter 8).

In other words, there has been a concentration of literature not only at the two extremes, but also on the first row of our table. This focus of the literature can only be explained by observing how profoundly the idea that leisure, and not directly work, affects welfare is rooted in the methodology of economics.

We saw in chapter 6 (section 4) that Robbins dismissed the importance of the Austro-English debate about the role of the disutility of labour on the grounds that work could be treated as forgone leisure (as Walras had implicitly suggested). Robbins himself gave the most widely accepted definition of economics; he maintained that it is 'the science which studies human behaviour as a relationship between ends and scarce means which have alternative uses' (1952, p. 16). Robbins wished to emphasize the fact that economists were concerned only with the relationship between ends and means. He believed that the definition of which variables should be taken as given by economists. 'ends as such', he added, 'do not form part of this subject matter. Nor does the technical and social environment. It is the relationship between these things and not the things in themselves which are important for the economist' (p. 38). And he added: 'That aspect of behaviour which is the subject matter of Economics is, as we have seen, conditioned by the scarcity of *given* means for the attainment of *given* ends' (p. 66).

Robbin's definition of economics implies that means and ends can be *given* and defined independently of their relationship – with the latter and not the former being the only concern of the economist. In particular, it is implicitly assumed in this definition that the variables that the economist studies show a peculiar kind of stability: they are either means or ends, and they never switch their role by crossing into intermediate stages in which they are both means and ends at the same time.

Consistent with the definition of economics, orthodox economic theory has divided human activities into two sets:

(1) leisure activities, which affect social welfare but do not affect production (i.e., they are only ends);
(2) work activities, which affect production but do not affect social welfare (i.e., they are only means).

Unfortunately, human activities do not fit into this rigid division. In particular, human activities can be productive (i.e., means for achieving certain ends) and at the same time can affect social welfare in general for the simple reason that human beings are performing them.

We can contrast the orthodox view of human work with Marx's definition of work, which we examined in the framework of a simple model in chapter 4. Whereas orthodox economics assumes that only leisure activities can be ends in themselves, Marx does not make this restrictive assumption. Production activities can be 'chosen activities' within a Marxian framework. And whereas, in a Marxian framework, work is endogenously defined as a deficit of necessary activities (given society's tastes and a state of technology), in the orthodox framework, work is exogenously defined as that set of human activities that affect production and not welfare. Finally, the homogeneity of work (i.e., the fact that workers are indifferent to the different uses of their labour in production) is justified by Marx by referring to a particular institutional framework in which the profit-maximizing behaviour of capitalists has rendered each job de-skilled and similar to other jobs. By contrast, the indifference of workers to the particular use of their manpower in production is implicitly assumed by orthodox economic theory. We might think that orthodox economists consider it unnecessary to point out that under capitalism work is abstract and alienated. But this is not the case. In welfare economics (when they also use the same assumption) the issue is how a society could be best organized, and not how it is actually organized under capitalism.

Arrow has given a definition of rationality which is actually the same definition that Robbins gives of economics. 'Rationality, after all,' he maintains, 'has to do with ends and means and their relation. It does not specify what the ends are. It only tries to make us aware of the congruence or dissonance between the two' (1974, p. 17). And Arrow has also rather proudly observed that 'An economist by training thinks of himself as the guardian of rationality, the ascriber of rationality to others, and the prescriber of rationality to the social world' (p. 16).

I myself have nothing against a subject that deals with the relation between ends and means, whether it is called 'rationality' or 'economics'. But if this relation is interpreted in the unnecessarily restrictive way that means cannot also be ends, prescribing and ascribing rationality to others, this can turn the economist into a modern version of a conservative priest – a role to which I profoundly object. Conservative priests used to prescribe the status quo by saying that life itself was a means to a superior end existing somewhere in the sky; economists would assume a similar role by maintaining that working life is simply a means to a superior end, existing somewhere on earth, called consumption goods and leisure. But our working life affects our welfare as much as our non-working life and the availability of consumption goods.

The rational prescriptions of orthodox economics imply that the authority of an efficient, profit-maximizing manager can be disputed only by irrational workers, and in this way they make the issue of industrial democracy and workers' control over working life an empty issue.

By contrast, the extension of democracy to the workplace is no longer an empty issue if we explicitly state that firms exist and workers derive (dis)utility from the uses of their labour-power. Quite surprisingly, not only orthodox economics but also the self-management literature has often failed to make these two points explicit. The theory of self-management (in both the better known Ward–Vanek–Meade and the less known Hertzka–Breit–Lange versions[2]) has considered the case of a competitive market economy but has failed to stress the 'incompleteness' of these markets. However, self-management can be correctly conceptualized in a situation where markets do not and cannot (because of the transaction cost argument) completely coordinate economic activity, particularly the allocation of labour. In a situation of complete markets the issue of self-management cannot arise, for the simple reason that in that situation nobody has to manage anybody else; in other words, in a situation of complete markets, firms do not really exist, with the obvious consequence that their (self-) management cannot be considered.

Moreover, the self-management literature has usually assumed that the members of the cooperatives maximize their income but not the utility that they derive from their work. This is tantamount to assuming that the workers have no preference for the allocation of their work and regard it only as a source of income. But if we accept this assumption, we necessarily come to the conclusion that the members of a self-managed firm will allocate their labour and manage themselves according to the same criterion by which a profit-maximizing employer will manage them.[3] And this conclusion makes the case for self-management unnecessarily weak.

By contrast, we have seen how joining together the assumptions that firms exist and that workers derive (dis)utility from the different tasks yields the conclusion that the extension of democracy to the workplace can bring about an organization of work superior to that achieved by a profit-maximizing employer.[4]

This conclusion is not meant to hide the very difficult problems that self-management and industrial democracy still have to face in both theory and practice. The need to take workers' preferences into account is an important argument in favour of self-management and industrial democracy; but it also implies that taking decisions in a self-managed firm is not so simple as the income-maximization or profit-maximization models suggest. Taking the objective function of a cooperative as given may be useful for simplifying the analysis, but it must be emphasized that the existence of workers' preferences implies that individuals with different preferences and different needs must find acceptable compromises within the self-managed firms. Aggregating preferences and finding common goals is not an easy task, either in theory or in practice. Taking decisions can be difficult and costly; it involves spending time at meetings and finding some mechanism of representative democracy for saving time and energy. Moreover, decisions must not only be taken, but must also be implemented and enforced. This implies that cooperatives have to find a form of organization by which a certain internal discipline can be established and potential free-riders can be kept under control.

But it would be misleading to compare a cooperative facing these real-life problems with an idealized textbook type of profit-maximizing firm whose managers allocate jobs and make people work as if they were machines. In a real-life capitalist firm the employers (as in orthodox economic theory) may not (or may not wish) to consider the preferences of workers and their goal of deriving utility from their working time; hence they may choose that organization of production which maximizes the revenue of work. But the workers are quite likely to pay attention to their own utility rather than to the goals of the employers. This implies that a real-life capitalist firm is characterized by a conflict of goals between employers and employees. Whereas the utility and the revenue of work are both likely to be goals of each member of a cooperative, in a capitalist firm these two goals usually 'belong' to two different classes of agents.

We have characterized the objective function of a cooperative which allocates a certain amount of labour-time in the following way:

$$U_i(x_i) + \lambda_i y_i$$

where $U_i(x_i)$ and $\lambda_i y_i$ are, respectively, the utility and the revenue of work (see sections 2.1 and 2.2 above). This objective function is 'split' into two objective functions in a capitalist firm. The first, $U_i(x_i)$, is the objective function of the workers; the second, $\lambda_i y_i$, is the objective function of the employers. The workers will try to perform those tasks that maximize the utility of the labour-time that they have agreed to perform for the employers. The employers will try to make the workers perform those tasks that maximize the revenue of work and, therefore, their profits.

Thus, the utility and the revenue of work, the two goals internalized by each member of a cooperative, often become the conflicting objectives of employers and employees in a capitalist firm. Of course, even in a cooperative the existence of these two goals can be a source of discussion and disagreement, because its members may give different degrees of importance to each of them; but in a cooperative each member is likely to give some degree of importance to both goals, and this circumstance eliminates the possibility of a polarized conflict of interests. By constrast, a polarized conflict of interests is quite likely to occur in a firm founded on the institution of the employment contract. Indeed, it is common experience that, after the employment contract has been signed and a wage has been agreed, employers and employees complain and sometimes struggle, for two conflicting sets of reasons. The employers usually complain about the low productivity of work, the fact that the workers do not put sufficient effort into carrying out their tasks, or the fact that the mobility of work within the firm is too low. In other words, they claim that the task levels and the types of tasks performed by the employees are not satisfactory. By contrast, the employees complain about the hardship, the disagreeableness and the boring and uninteresting nature of the tasks to which they have been assigned.

This goal incongruence between employers and employees that characterizes real-life capitalist firms is likely to result in a much more costly factory than any democratic or monitoring procedure that might characterize a self-managed firm.

The fact that the employers may not take into account the workers' preferences may imply that the organization of work is characterized by uninteresting and de-skilled jobs.[5] If this is the nature of their jobs, and if the revenue of the firm is not their goal, then the workers will have a strong incentive to shirk. This implies that a capitalist firm will have to monitor not simply the few 'anti-social' free-riders who are likely to exist in a self-managed firm, but a whole workforce which has a tendency to shirk. Moreover, in such a situation the control that the majority of workers in a cooperative may exercise on the 'anti-social' shirkers may well be replaced by active support for workers caught 'shirking' by the employers. A capitalist firm, therefore, will probably have to employ many people to monitor other people instead of producing useful goods; it will probably also have to introduce unsatisfactory and costly division of labour which favours monitoring.[6] A cooperative where the workers rightly see the revenue of work as their own goal is quite likely to have lower monitoring costs. Moreover, within a capitalist firm monitoring is effective only if there is considerable penalty for the worker who, caught shirking, is fired. But this penalty is very slight in a situation of relatively full employment; in fact, in an idealized situation of full employment, where it is assumed that transaction costs do not exist, this penalty can be said to be nil, because a worker who is fired by an employer can immediately find a job in another firm. Hence, unemployment is a necessary evil in a capitalist system. It is a necessary consequence of the goal incongruence between employers and employees, and follows from the fact that, without its threat, the employees may have no incentive for working.[7] By contrast, the workers of a self-managed economy, where they feel that both the utility and the revenue of work are their own goals, may well find this threat unnecessary; and hence the need for unemployment would become redundant. In other words, unemployment is to be added to other costs that arise from the conflict of goals between employers and employees. And unemployment is very costly for society, not only because it implies that some valuable human resources are involuntarily idle, but also because it makes the 'exit' mechanism very costly for the workers, increasing the already considerable costs of expressing their preferences by this mechanism and causing a deterioration of working conditions. (On this point, see chapter 3 and esp. n. 3.)

In spite of the prescriptions and the consequences of orthodox economics, the extension of democracy to the workplace is a very substantial issue. It is important because, quite apart from its convenience in allowing society to overcome the costly consequences of the conflict between employers and employees (or 'socialist' profit-maximizing managers and workers), democracy may well be an end in itself. It is also important because effective workers' control over decision-making implies choices of different forms of organization of labour and different techniques of production; and in the longer run, this could contribute towards the development of new techniques of production. If the workers have the power to shape the organization of production, then they can shape it in such a way that it takes into account the needs of people as producers. And this is of vital importance if work is to become less and less a source of distress and more and more a source of welfare.

Notes

1 Left and right here are typographical rather than political categories!
2 Ward (1958), Vanek (1980) and Meade (1972) consider a model in which cooperatives choose their membership according to the income-per-head maximizing rule. This implies that in equilibrium the marginal productivity of labour in a cooperative must equal its average income. This condition has some perverse consequences, since it implies that cooperatives increase (decrease) their membership when there is excess supply (demand) for their product. It is probably for this reason that this stream of the self-management literature has largely concentrated on the (perverse) market reactions of a self-managed economy, rather than on the characteristics of the internal organization of the self-managed firm. On the other hand, these perverse reactions do not

characterize a pre-existing model of the self-managed economy proposed by Hertzka (1905) and Breit and Lange (1982). The characteristic of this second model is that the firms must always accept every worker who wants to become a member, and thus cannot choose their membership according to the rule of maximizing income per head. In this model the 'perverse' reactions that characterize the Ward–Vanek–Meade model are obviously overcome, but new problems arise. On this matter see Chilosi (1982), Cugno (1983), Ferrero (1983), Nuti (1983) and Pagano (1984).

3 This can be easily proved by observing that in this literature a cooperative is assumed to maximize the income per head

$$z_i = \frac{\lambda_i y_i}{N_i}$$

where

$$N_i = \sum_{ij} x_{ij}$$

is the number of workers employed in the cooperative i and where

$$y_i = f_i(x_i, \ldots, x_t).$$

Maximizing z_i yields the following first-order optimality conditions:

$$\frac{\partial z_i}{\partial x_{ij}} = \frac{\lambda_i \dfrac{\partial f_i}{\partial x_{ij}} N_i - \lambda_t y_i}{N_i^2} = 0 \quad j = 1, \ldots, T$$

from which

$$\lambda \frac{\partial f_i}{\partial x_{ij}} = \frac{\lambda_i y_i}{N_i} = z \quad j = 1, \ldots, T$$

and therefore

$$\frac{\partial f_i}{\partial x_{i1}} = \frac{\partial f_i}{\partial x_{i2}} = \ldots = \frac{\partial f_i}{\partial x_{iT}}$$

which is identical to rule (5.3) of chapter 7, which is applied by a profit-maximizing manager.

By contrast, we have assumed that the members of a cooperative maximize the sum of the utility of work and the difference between revenue and costs of work (measured at shadow price of labour power). If we believe that these shadow prices do not exist, we may assume that a cooperative maximizes the sum of the revenue and the utility that is derived from one unit of labour-power. In this case the objective function of a cooperative would be a function T such that

$$T = \frac{U_i(x_i) + \lambda_i y_i}{N_i}.$$

Maximizing T would yield the following necessary conditions for optimality:

$$\frac{\partial T}{\partial x_{ij}} = \frac{\lambda_i \dfrac{\partial f^i}{\partial x_{ij}} N_i - \lambda_i y_i + \dfrac{\partial U}{\partial x_{ij}} N - U_i(x_i)}{N_i^2} = 0 \quad j = 1, \dots, T$$

and therefore

$$\lambda_i \frac{\partial f^i}{\partial x_{ij}} + \frac{\partial U_i}{\partial x_{ij}} = \frac{\lambda_i y_i + U_i(x_i)}{N_i} = T \quad j = 1, \dots, T$$

from which, under assumption 2.1 in this chapter, we can re-obtain condition (5.7) of chapter 7. The relevant difference is that we assume explicitly that a cooperative internalizes the utility function of the workers; in other words, given a certain amount of labour-power

$$L_i = \sum_j x_{ij}$$

the cooperative maximizes a function $U_i(x_i) + \lambda_i y_i$ and not simply $\lambda_i y_i$.

4 Dreze (1976) and Dreze and Hagen (1978) have suggested that the choice of working conditions can be treated in the same way as the choice of the quality of consumption goods. In both cases they come to the interesting conclusion that the market is efficient only if the number of goods is greater than the number of characteristics. However, it seems to me that their analysis misses one important difference between the product market and the labour market. The former is usually organized by sales contracts, whereas the latter is often organized by employment contracts. In the case of employment contracts, the most important issue is not the possibility or impossibility of computing a 'sufficient' set of characteristics from a complete set of traded commodities, but the implication that the set of traded commodities is incomplete. In other words, the existence of firms implies that some task or intermediate product markets do not exist. In the present work it is the existence of firms that implies that workers' self-management can improve working conditions, whereas in Dieze's and Hagen's papers it is the impossibility of computing the prices of characteristics which leads to the same conclusion. Also, Vanek (1969) and Horvat (1982) stress (although for different reasons) the importance of self-management for improving working conditions. The importance of industrial democracy is very well underlined in Edwards (1979).

5 This is not the only possibility. The employees may successfully struggle to have (some of) their preferences taken into account by the employers and the employers may sometimes be willing to 'internalize' (some) preferences of (some groups) of workers in their objective function. In this way the employers may increase the productivity of labour by involving the workers in more interesting jobs and in some aspects of

decision-making. (On this point see n. 1, chapter 1.) This behaviour distinguishes the 'participatory' firm from the traditional capitalist firm considered in this paragraph.

6   Reich and Devine (1981) believe that self-management can improve working conditions because it reduces monitoring costs. Monitoring, it is maintained, implies a very minute and unsatisfactory division of labour in a capitalist firm, which could be avoided in a cooperative. While I share their view on this point, I think that it is important to emphasize that working conditions can improve under self-management quite independently of the monitoring costs argument, for the simple reason that the maximand of a self-managed firm is different from that of a capitalist firm. While the former internalizes the goal of maximizing the utility of work, the managers of the latter may simply organize work according to the profit-maximizing rule. And we have seen in chapter 7 that profit-maximization implies the choice of a de-skilled and detailed division of labour which may well be changed by self-management.

7   Shapiro and Stiglitz (1984) have shown how (incomplete) monitoring implies that the equilibrium of a market economy requires unemployment 'as a worker discipline device'. 'Under the conventional competitive paradigm,' they argue, 'in which all workers receive the market wage and there is no unemployment, the worst that can happen to a worker who shirks is that he is fired. Since he can immediately be rehired, however, he pays no penalty for his misdemeanour. With imperfect monitoring and full employment, therefore, workers will choose to shirk.' Shapiro's and Stiglitz's contribution is very interesting. However, they fail to mention that such widespread shirking will occur only if the workers have the objective functions used in their model. These objective functions are the outcome of a situation in which the workers do not share the goals of the managers of the firm where they work. They are likely to characterize (some of) the workers in a capitalist firm, but they may well change under alternative institutions such as a self-managed firm. This point is very well argued in Bowles and Gintis (1983).

References

Arrow, K. J. (1959) 'Toward a Theory of Price Adjustment', in K. J. Arrow and L. Hurwicz (eds) (1977) *Studies in Resource Allocation Processes*, Cambridge, Cambridge University Press.

Arrow, K. J. (1974) *The Limits of Organization*, New York, W. W. Norton.

Arrow, K. J. (1979) 'The Division of Labour in the Economy, the Polity and the Society', in G. P. O'Driscoll (ed.) *A. Smith and Modern Political Economy*, Ames, Iowa State University Press.

Arrow, K. H. and Hahn, F. H. (1971) *General Competitive Analysis*, San Francisco and Edinburgh, Oliver & Boyd.

Arrow, K. J. and Hurwicz, L. (1960) 'Decentralization and Computation in Resource Allocation', in K. J. Arrow and L. Hurwicz (eds) (1977) *Studies in Resource Allocation Processes*, Cambridge, Cambridge University Press.

Arrow, K. J. and Hurwicz, L. (eds) (1977) *Studies in Resource Allocation Processes*, Cambridge, Cambridge University Press.

Babbage, C. (1832) *On the Economy of Machinery and Manufactures*, London, Charles Knight.

Barone, E. (1908) 'The Ministry of Production in the Collectivist State', in A. Nove and D. M. Nuti (eds) (1972) *Socialist Economics*, Harmondsworth, Penguin.

Batt, W. (1933) *The Law of the Master and the Servant*, London, Pitman and Sons.

Blaug, M. (1972) *Economic Theory in Retrospect*, London, Heinemann.

Böhm-Bawerk, E. (1894a) 'The Ultimate Standard of Value', *Annals of the American Academy of Political and Social Science*, vol. 5, pp. 149-208.

Böhm-Bawerk, E. (1894b) 'One Word More on the Ultimate Standard of Value', *Economic Journal*, vol. 4, pp. 719-24.

Böhm-Bawerk, E. (1959) *Capital and Interest*, vol. II, *Positive Theory of Capital*, Libertarian Press, South Holland, Illinois.

Bowles, S. and Gintis, H. (1983) 'The Power of Capital: On the Inadequacy of the Conception of the Capitalistic Economy as Private', *Philophical Forum*, vol. 14, pp. 225-45.

Braverman, H. (1974) *Labour and Monopoly Capital*, New York, Monthly Review Press.

Bray, J. F. (1839) *Labour's Wrongs and Labour's Remedy, or The Age of Might and the Age of Right*, Leeds.

Breit, M. and Lange, D. (1982) 'Un modello di economia socialista autogestita con garanzia di pieno impiego e di uguaglianza distributiva', *Rivista Internazionale di Scienze Sociali*, vol. 90, pp. 301-4.

Chilosi, A. (1982) 'Il modello di economia socialista di mercato autogestita di Breit e Lange', *Rivista Internazionale di Scienze Sociali*, vol. 90, pp. 298-300.

Coase, R. H. (1953) 'The Nature of the Firm', *Economica*, 1937; republished in G. J. Stigler and K. E. Boulding (eds), *Readings in Price Theory*, New York, George Allen & Unwin.

Cohen, G. S. (1981) 'Managers and Machinery: An Analysis of the Rise of Factory Production', *Australian Economic Papers*, vol. 20, pp. 24-41.

Cugno, F. (1983) 'L'Impresa e il mercato in un'economia con diritto dei lavoratori ad essere assunti', *Rivista Internazionale di Scienze Sociali*, vol. 91, pp. 296-304.

Dobb, M. H. (1933) 'Economic Theory and the Problem of a Socialist Economy', *Economic Journal*, 19 December, pp. 588-98.

Dobb, M. H. (1935) 'Economic Theory and Socialist Economy: A Reply', *Review of Economic Studies*, vol. 3, pp. 144-51.

Dreze, S. H. (1976) 'Some Theory of Labor Management and Participation', *Econometrica*, vol. 44, pp. 1125-39.

Dreze, S. H. and Hagen, P. K. (1978) 'Choice of Produce Quality: Equilibrium and Efficiency', *Econometrica*, vol. 4, pp. 493-513.

Edgeworth, F. Y. (1894) 'One Word More on the Ultimate Standard of Value: Reply to Böhm-Bawerk', *Economic Journal*, vol. 4, pp. 724-5.

Edgeworth, F. Y. (1925) *Papers Relating to Political Economy*, vol. III, London, Macmillan.

Edwards, R. (1979) *Contested Terrain*, New York, Basic Books.

Farrel, M. C. (1973) *Readings in Welfare Economics*, London, Macmillan.

Ferrero, M. (1983) 'L'Economia utopistica di Theodor Hertzka e il problema della giustizia nei sistemi economici', *Rivista Internazionale di Scienze Sociali*, vol. 91, pp. 251-95.

Friedman, A. L. (1977) *Industry and Labour*, London and Basingstoke, Macmillan.

Fritzroy, F. R. (1978) 'Alienation, Freedom and Economic Organisation', *Acton Society Trust Occasional Papers*, Siena Series no. 10, London.

Ginsburg, A. (1976) *I Socialisti Ricardiani*, Turin, Isedi.

Gintis, H. (1976) 'The Nature of Labour Exchange and the Theory of Capitalist Production', *Review of Radical Political Economics*, vol. 8, pp. 36-54.

Gioia, M. (1815) *Nuovo Prospetto Delle Scienze Economiche*, vol. I, Lugano, Presso Guis, Ruggia.

Goreux, L. M. and Manne, A. S. (eds) (1973) *Multilevel Planning: Case Studies in Mexico*, Amsterdam, North-Holland.

Gray, J. (1825) *A Lecture on Human Happiness*, London, LSE Reprints.

Gray, J. (1831) *The Social System*, London.

Gray, J. (1848) *Lectures on Money*, Clifton, NH, Library of Money and Banking History Reprints.

Hayek, F. A. (1935) *Collectivist Economic Planning*, London, Routledge.

Heal, G. M. (1973) *The Theory of Economic Planning*, Amsterdam, North Holland.

Hertzka, T. (1905) *A Trip to Freeland*, Washington, Bow.

Hirschman, A. D. (1970) *Exit, Voice and Loyalty*, Cambridge, Mass., Harvard University Press.

Hodgskin, T. (1825) *Labour Defended against the Claims of Capital, London*.

Hodgskin, T. (1827) *Popular Political Economy*, London, Charles Tait.

Horvat, B. (1982) Labour-managed Firms and Social Transformation in F. H. Stephen (ed.), *Performance of Labour-managed Firms*, London and Basingstoke, Macmillan.

Jaffé, W. (1967) 'Walras's Theory of Tatonnement: A Critique of Recent Interpretations', *Journal of Political Economy*, vol. 75, pp. 1-19.

Jaffé, W. (1975) 'Leon Walras, an Economic Adviser Manquee', *Economic Journal*, vol. 85, pp. 810-23.

Jaffé, W. (1977) 'The Normative Bias of the Walrasian Model: Walras versus Gossen', *Quarterly Journal of Economics*, vol. 91, pp. 371-87.

Jaffé, W. (1978) 'Review of Michio Morishima's Walras's Economics: A Pure Theory of Capital and Money', *Economic Journal*, vol. 88, pp. 574-6.

Jaffé, W. (1980) 'Walras's Economics As Others See It', *Journal of Economic Literature*, vol. 18, pp. 528-49.

Jevons, W. S. (1968) *The State in Relation to Labour*, New York, Augustus M. Kelley.

Jevons, W. S. (1970) *The Theory of Political Economy*, intr. Collison Black, Harmondsworth, Penguin.

Kant, E. (1949) 'Metaphysical Foundations of Morals', in C. J. Friedrich (ed.), *The Philosophy of Kant*, New York, Modern Library.

Koopmans, T. C. (1951) 'Analysis of Production as an Efficient Combination of Activities', in *Activity Analysis of Production and Allocation*, New York, John Wiley.

Kornai, J. (1971) *Anti-equilibrium. On the Economic Systems Theory and the Tasks of Research*, Amsterdam, North-Holland.

Kornai, J. (1973) 'Thoughts on Multi-level Planning Systems', in L. M. Goreux and A. S. Manne (eds), *Multilevel Planning: Case Studies in Mexico*, Amsterdam, North Holland.

Kornai, J. and Liptak, K. T. (1963) 'Two-level Planning', *Econometrica*, vol. 33, pp. 141-69.

Lange, O. (1936) 'On the Economic Theory of Socialism: Part I', *Review of Economic Studies*, vol. 4, pp. 53-71; reprinted in Farrel (1973).

Littler, C. R. (1982) *The Development of the Labour Process in Capitalist Societies*, London, Heinemann.

Lowenthal, E. (1911). 'The Ricardian Socialists', PhD thesis, *Columbia University Studies in History, Economics (etc.)*, vol. 46i.

Macvane (1890) 'Böhm-Bawerk on Value and Wages', *Quarterley Journal of Economics.*

Makowski, L. (1979) 'A General Equilibrium Theory of Organization', University of Cambridge, Economics Theory Discussion Paper no. 12.

Malinvaud, E. (1967) 'Decentralized Procedures for Planning' in E. Malinvaud and M. Bacharach (eds), *Activity Analysis in the Theory of Growth and Planning*, London, Macmillan.

Marglin, S. (1974) 'What Do Bosses Do?' *Review of Radical Political Economy*, vol. 6, pp. 60–112.

Marshall, A. (1885) 'The Present Position of Economics', in A. C. Pigou (ed.) (1925) *Memorials of Alfred Marshall*, London, Macmillan.

Marshall, A. (1890) *Some Aspects of Competition*, Leeds; reprinted in R. L. Smyth (ed.), *Essays in the Economics of Socialism and Capitalism*, London, Gerald Duckworth, 1964.

Marshall, A. (1979) *Principles of Economics*, London, Macmillan.

Marx, K. (1955) *The Poverty of Philosophy*, Moscow, Foreign Languages Publishing House.

Marx, K. (1967) *Capital*, New York, International Publishers.

Marx, K. (1968) 'Introduction to the "Critique of Political Economy"', in D. Horowitz (ed.), *Marx and Modern Economics*, New York, Monthly Review Press.

Marx, K. (1975) 'Economic and Philosophical Manuscripts', in *Early Writings*, intr. L. Colletti, Harmondsworth, Penguin.

Marx, K. (1978) 'Critique to the Gotha Programme', in T. Borodulina (ed.), *Marx, Engels, Lenin on Communist Society*, Moscow, Progress Publishers.

Meade, J. E. (1972) 'The Theory of Labour-managed Firms and Profit-sharing', *Economic Journal*, vol. 82, pp. 402–28.

Menger, A. (1899) *The Right to the Whole Produce of Labour*, London.

Menger, C. (1950) *Principles of Economics*, Glencoe, Ill., Free Press.

Menger, C. (1963) *Problems of Economics and Sociology*, ed. and intr. Louis Schneider, Urbana, Ill., University of Illinois Press.

Menger, K. (1973) 'Austrian Marginalism and Mathematical Economics', in J. Hicks and W. Weber (eds), *Carl Menger and the Austrial School of Economics*, Oxford, Clarendon Press.

Mill, J. S. (1844) *Elements of Political Economy*, London, Henry G. Bohn.

Mises, L. von (1920) 'Economic Calculation in the Socialist Commonwealth', in A. Nove and D. M. Nuti (eds) (1972) *Socialist Economics*, Harmondsworth, Penguin.

Morishima, M. (1977) *Walras's Economics: A Pure Theory of Capital and Money*, Cambridge and New York, Cambridge University Press.

Nove, A. and Nuti, D. M. (eds) (1972) *Socialist Economics*, Harmondsworth, Penguin.

Nuti, D. M. (1983) 'Fusioni ed efficienza nei modelli di economie autogestite', *Rivista Internazionale di Scienze Sociali*, vol. 91, pp. 487–95.

Owen, R. (1970) *Report to the County of Lanark*, Harmondsworth, Penguin.

Pagano, U. (1975) 'How Can Some Decisions of a Socialist Society by Decentralized to Firms', dissertation submitted for the Economic Tripos Part II at the Faculty of Economics, University of Cambridge.

Pagano, U. (1978a) 'Alcuni Commenti Su Lavoro e Capitale Monopolistico di H. Braverman', *Quaderni Piacentini*, vol. 69, pp. 91-101.

Pagano, U. (1978b) 'Teoria Neoclassica, Pianificazione e Marxismo', *Note Economische*, no. 2, pp. 100-19.

Pagano, U. (1980) 'Workers' Preferences, and the Organization of Production in Resource Allocation Models', University of Cambridge, Faculty of Economics and Politics, Research Paper no. 13.

Pagano, U. (1981) 'The Austro-English Opportunity-Pain-Cost Controversy', Paper given at the CNR seminar, Siena, June 1981 (mimeo).

Pagano, U. (1983) 'Profit Maximization, Industrial Democracy and the Allocation of Labour', *The Manchester School*, no. 2, pp. 159-83.

Pagano, U. (1984) 'Occupazione ed Autogestione. Una Alternativa Intermedia', *Rivista Internazionale di Scienze Sociali* (in press).

Pareto, V. (1896) *Cours d'economie politique*, Lausanne.

Pasinetti, L. L. (1977) *Lectures on the Theory of Production*, London, Macmillan.

Pratten, C. F. (1980) 'The Manufacture of Pins', *Journal of Economic Literature*, vol. 18, pp. 93-6.

Reich, M. and Devine, D. (1981) 'The Microeconomics of Conflict and Hierarchy in Capitalist Production', *Review of Radical Political Economy*, vol. 12, pp. 27-45.

Ricardo, D. (1953) 'Notes on Malthus's Principles of Political Economy', in P. Sraffa (ed.) *The Works and Correspondence of David Ricardo*, Cambridge, Cambridge University Press.

Ricardo, D. (1971) *On the Principles of Political Economy and Taxation*, Harmondsworth, Penguin.

Robbins, L. (1930), 'The Conception of Stationary Equilibrium', *Economic Journal*, vol. 40, pp. 194-214.

Robbins, L. (1936) 'The Place of Jevons in the History of Economic Thought', *The Manchester School*, vol. 7, pp. 1-17.

Robbins, L. (1952) *An Essay on the Nature and the Significance of Economic Science*, London, Macmillan.

Robbins, L. (1970) *The Evolution of Modern Economic Theory and other Papers on the History of Economic Thought*, Edinburgh, Macmillan.

Robertson, D. H. (1928) *The Control of Industry*, Cambridge, Cambridge University Press.

Rowthorn, R. (1974) 'Neo-Classicism, Neo-Ricardianism and Marxism', *New Left Review*, vol. 86, pp. 63-82.

Sabel, C. F. (1982) *Work and Politics*, Cambridge, Cambridge University Press.

Schumpeter, J. A. (1953) *History of Economic Analysis*, Boston and Sydney, George Allen & Unwin.

186

Sen, A. K. (1975) 'On the Concept of Economic Efficiency', in M. Parkin and A. R. Nobay (eds), *Contemporary Issues in Economics*, Manchester, Manchester University Press.

Shapiro, C. and Stiglitz, J. E. (1984) 'Equilibrium Unemployment as a Worker Discipline Device', *American Economic Review*, vol. 74, pp. 433-44.

Simon, H. A. (1957) *Models of Man*, chapters 10 and 11, New York, John Wiley.

Smart, W. (1892) *An Introduction to the Theory of Value, on the Lines of Menger, Wieser and Böhm-Bawerk*, London, Macmillan.

Smith, A. (1976) *An Inquiry into the Nature and Causes of the Wealth of Nations*, ed. E. Cannan, Chicago, University of Chicago Press.

Stigler, G. (1968) *Production and Distribution Theories*, New York, Agathon Press.

Thompson, N. (1981) 'The Popularization of Anti-capitalist and Socialist Political Economy in the Working-class Press, 1816-34', PhD thesis, University of Cambridge.

Thompson, W. (1827) *Labour Rewarded*, London.

Ure, A. (1835) *The Philosophy of Manufactures*, London, Charles Knight.

Uzawa, H. (1958) 'Iterative Methods for Concave Programming', chapter 10 of K. Arrow, K. J. Hurwicz and H. Uzawa, *Studies in Linear and Non-linear Programming*, Stanford, Stanford University Press.

Vanek, D. (1969) 'Decentralization under Workers' Management: A Theoretical Appraisal', in D. Vanek (ed.), *Self-Management: Economic Liberation of Man*, Harmondsworth, Penguin.

Vanek, D. (1970) *The General Theory of Labour-managed Market Economies*, Ithaca, Cornell University Press.

Walras, L. (1896) *Etudes D'Economie Sociale (Théorie de la Repartition de la Richesse Sociale)*, Lausanne, F. Rouge/Paris, F. Pichon.

Walras, L. (1898) *Etudes D'Economie Politique Appliqueé (Théorie de la Production de la Richesse Sociale)*, Lausanne, F. Rouge/Paris, F. Pichon.

Walras, L. (1977) *Elements of Pure Economics, or The Theory of Social Wealth*, tran. W. Jaffé, Fairfield, Conn., Augustus M. Kelley.

Ward, B. M. (1958) 'The Firm in Illyria: Market Syndicalism', *American Economic Review*, vol. 48, pp. 566-89.

Wieser, von F. (1892) 'The Theory of Value', *Annals of the American Academy*, March, pp. 21-52.

Wieser, von F. (1893) *Natural Value*, London, Macmillan.

Williamson, O. E. (1975) *Markets and Hierarchies: Analysis and Antitrust Implications. A Study in the Economics of Internal Organization.* New York, Free Press.

Zamagni, S. (1982) 'Sui Fondamenti Metodologici della Scuola Austriaca', *Note Economiche*, no. 3, pp. 63-93.

Index

187